华东师范大学出版社

GUO JI SHANG WU YING YU HAN DIAN

国际商务英语函电

职 业 学 校 商 贸、财 经 专 业 教 学 用 书

主 编 沙 佩
副主编 朱红萍 王炳章

U0330934

出版说明

　　本书是职业学校国际商务专业的教学用书。本书采用情景导入、任务引领、项目驱动的编写方法，以实际案例进行操练。内容与职业学校学生的认知特点和岗位技能要求相适应，表现形式灵活多样、新颖别致。

　　本书共有 12 个单元。每个单元的具体栏目设计如下：

　　Situational Introduction 情景介绍　　以职校学生李娜在外贸公司实习的模拟情景引入各单元的主要内容。

　　Knowledge to Impart 知识传授　　通过对话或实例的形式，教授各单元的主要知识。

　　Practice 小练习　　辅以与"小知识"内容紧密相扣的练习题，便于学生即学即用。

　　Comments & Suggestions 评价及建议　　评价学生对本单元知识的掌握程度，并要求学生熟记词汇。

　　Knowledge Consolidation 知识点巩固　　综合应用练习，使学生通过完成此练习达到巩固知识的目的。

　　为了方便教师的教学活动，本书还配套有：

　　《国际商务英语函电·教师手册》　　含有各单元的教学目标、任务分析、教学内容拓展以及教材练习的参考答案等，便于教师备课、组织课堂教学。

华东师范大学出版社

中等职业教育分社

2012 年 12 月

前　言

QIANYAN

随着我国加入 WTO,国际贸易得到了迅速发展,对外联系和信息交流日趋频繁。作为对外交流的一种主要方式,商务英语函电在国际贸易活动中起到了至关重要的作用。"商务英语函电"是职业学校国际商务专业的一门主要课程,本课程的教学目的是培养学生能用英语处理进出口业务中的一般商务往来函电、签订合同和填写相关单据,同时帮助该专业的学生掌握有关国际贸易函电的写作技巧及与国际商务活动相关的词汇、句型以及专业知识,使学生成为高素质的中级应用型技术人才。

为此,结合职业教育课改的发展方向,我们编写了《国际商务英语函电》。本教材共有 12 个单元,3 个附录。每个单元主题突出,分别介绍了商务信函的写作方法、商务信函的格式、如何建立业务关系、询盘及回复、报盘与还盘、订单与合同、支付方式、信用证、包装、保险、运输以及投诉与处理。

本教材的编写以充分调动和激发学生的学习积极性为宗旨,打破了传统专业英语教材的格局,注重实用性、时代性、连贯性和职业性,每个单元内容重点明确,格调新颖,语言简洁、通俗易懂,使学生在未来的就业中对自己所学的知识能够做到管用、够用和实用。课文中所使用的词汇、短语和术语都是商务英语中频繁出现的。课文内容由浅入深,环环相扣,栏目设计生动活泼,引人入胜。本书的编写采用情景导入、任务引领、项目驱动和模块式的写作手段,以实际案例进行操练。本书适合职业学校国际商务专业的学生使用,也可作为有志从事对外贸易行业人士的自学用书。

本书由沙佩担任主编。参加本书编写的有:沙佩(Unit 1~3),朱红萍(Unit 4~8),王炳章(Unit 9~12)。全书由沙佩撰写大纲并进行统稿。在编写过程中,编者参阅了大量的相关专业文献和著作。在此,编者对在本书编写过程中给予帮助的各位专家、学者和同仁表示衷心的感谢。由于编者的水平有限,书中的错误和不足之处在所难免,敬请读者批评指正。

编　者

2012 年 12 月

Contents

Unit 1   Essential Qualities of Writing Business Letters   1

Unit 2   Layout of a Business Letter   7

Unit 3   Establishing Business Relations   19

Unit 4   Enquiries and Replies   31

Unit 5   Offers and Counter-offers   41

Unit 6   Orders and Contracts   51

Unit 7   Payment   62

Unit 8   Letter of Credit   76

Unit 9   Packing   89

Unit 10   Insurance   100

Unit 11   Shipment   110

Unit 12   Claims & Settlement   120

Appendix I   New Words and Phrases to Each Unit   130

Appendix II   Phrases Commonly Used in Foreign Trade   145

Appendix III   Incoterms 2010 & 2000   153

References   154

Unit 1　Essential Qualities of Writing Business Letters

Situational Introduction 情景介绍

李娜是某职业学校商务英语专业二年级的学生，根据学校工学交替计划安排，本学期她被安排到一家外贸公司实习。张先生——她的带教老师，正在给她讲授有关国际贸易业务员跟单做货的知识。张先生说：要做好一票货，首先要学会跟客户交流和沟通。如何进行沟通呢？商务信函往来是商务活动的重要组成部分，是深思熟虑的产物，它能最大限度地减少电话和面谈中可能出现的疏漏和误解。接着，张先生与李娜探讨了书写商务信函的技巧。

Knowledge to Impart 知识传授

Mr. Zhang：Business communication is concerned with the successful exchange of messages that support the goal of buying and selling goods or other services. A good business letter can play an important role in trade，increase friendship and obtain complete understanding between the parties involved. Therefore，business letter writing is one of the necessary business activities. If you want to get a general idea about the essential qualities of writing a good business letter，you should always bear in mind the 7C's principles.

（商务沟通与成功地进行信息交流相关联，交流成功有助于实现货物买卖或其他劳务之目标。一封好的商务信函在交易中起着重要的作用，它可以增进友谊，使贸易相关方获得全面的了解。因此，商务信函的写作是必要的商务活动之一。假如你想了解有关书写一封好的商务信函的基本要素的话，请你牢记 7C 原则）

Li Na：What are they? Can you tell me in details?

Mr. Zhang：They are **Clearness，Conciseness，Consideration，Courtesy，Concreteness，Correctness，Completeness.**

　　Clearness means that your letter is clear and easy to understand. Therefore，you should choose plain，simple，familiar，conversational，straight-forward words.

　　Conciseness is considered the most important principle in business letter writing.

国际商务英语函电

To achieve conciseness, you should avoid wordy statement and fancy language; use short sentences instead of long ones; paragraph your message carefully.

Consideration means thoughtfulness. So you should always put yourself in your reader's place; keep in mind the receiver you are writing to; understand his or her problem and take the positive attitude.

Courtesy means the polite expression or kind action. You should be sincerely tactful and appreciative; take a personable, friendly and modest tone; be prompt in reply.

Concreteness: Business letters avoid being too general. You should use specific facts and figures, and try to use vivid and exact words.

Correctness: You should pay more attention to this principle, especially when you are giving information about dates, specifications, quantities, discounts, commission, units and figures, etc. A minor mistake in this respect sometimes will make you gain no profit or even lose out.

Completeness: A business letter is successful and functions well only when it contains all the necessary information your receiver expects. All the matters should be discussed and all the questions should be answered.

Li Na: Thank you for telling me so much. I will always keep in my mind the above-mentioned 7C's principles in business letter writing.
Mr. Zhang: Now I'd like you to do some practice according to what we have talked about.
Li Na: Let me try.

 Practice 小练习

Task 1: Answer the following questions.

1. What are the 7C's principles of writing business letters?

2. Which principle is the most important one in your opinion?

3. What's your weak point in the 7C's principles?

4. Is it necessary for us to study and master the basic knowledge of writing business letters?

国际商务英语函电

Task 2: Decide whether the following statements are true or false.

(　　) 1. Business communication has little to do with the successful exchange of messages that support the goal of buying and selling goods or other services.

(　　) 2. Keep your sentences short and eliminate excessive details.

(　　) 3. You must use the exact words in order to avoid the confusing idea.

(　　) 4. A concise letter must be a short one.

(　　) 5. Promptness is very important，because no one likes to wait for a long time before he gets a reply to his letter.

(　　) 6. A good business letter is essential in achieving good communication.

(　　) 7. To be concrete，we need to use specific figures and active verbs.

(　　) 8. As far as the language used concerned，the writing of a business letter is similar to the writing of a private letter.

Task 3: Choose the right answer for each sentence.

(　　) 1. "We cannot deliver the goods you ordered before next week." What principle does this sentence violate?
　　　A. Courtesy　　　　　　　　B. Conciseness
　　　C. Completeness　　　　　　D. Consideration

(　　) 2. "The goods will be sent to you in about 3 weeks." What principle does this sentence not obey?
　　　A. Courtesy　　　　　　　　B. Conciseness
　　　C. Completeness　　　　　　D. Concreteness

(　　) 3. We _____ the goods you offered in your last letter.
　　　A. interest　　　　　　　　B. are interested
　　　C. interest in　　　　　　　D. are interested in

(　　) 4. We hope you will find the shipment _____.
　　　A. orderly　　　　　　　　B. with order
　　　C. of order　　　　　　　　D. in order

(　　) 5. The sentence "Your letter is not clear at all. I can't understand it." violates the principle of _____.
　　　A. Courtesy　　　　　　　　B. Conciseness
　　　C. Completeness　　　　　　D. Clearness

(　　) 6. We are looking forward _____ your early reply.
　　　A. /　　　　　　　　　　　B. to receive
　　　C. receiving　　　　　　　　D. to receiving

国际商务英语函电

Comments & Suggestions 评价及建议

李娜出色地完成了三项任务,现在要求她熟练掌握以下单词与词组。

1. attitude [ˈætɪtjuːd] *n*. 态度
2. involve [ɪnˈvɒlv] *v*. 涉及
3. essential [ɪˈsenʃəl] *a*. 基本的
4. obtain [əbˈteɪn] *v*. 获得,取得, 得到
5. tactful [ˈtæktfəl] *a*. 得体的,圆滑的
6. clearness [ˈklɪənɪs] *n*. 清楚
7. conciseness [kənˈsaɪsnɪs] *n*. 简洁
8. consideration [kənˌsɪdəˈreɪʃən] *n*. 周到
9. courtesy [ˈkɜːtəsɪ] *n*. 礼貌
10. concreteness [ˈkɒnkriːtnɪs] *n*. 具体
11. correctness [kəˈrektnɪs] *n*. 正确
12. completeness [kəmˈpliːtnɪs] *n*. 完整
13. principle [ˈprɪnsəpl] *n*. 原则
14. positive [ˈpɒzɪtɪv] *a*. 主动的
15. conversational [ˌkɒnvəˈseɪʃnəl] *a*. 对话的
16. personable [ˈpɜːsənəbl] *a*. 优雅的,风度翩翩的,貌美的
17. specification [ˌspesɪfɪˈkeɪʃən] *n*. 规格
18. commission [kəˈmɪʃən] *n*. 佣金,手续费
19. appreciative [əˈpriːʃɪətɪv] *a*. 表示赞赏的,感谢的
20. prompt [prɒmpt] *a*. 敏捷的,及时的,迅速的

....

1. straight-forward words 易懂的话
2. wordy statement 啰唆的写法
3. fancy language 花哨的用词
4. bear in mind 牢记在心
5. modest tone 谦虚的口吻
6. be prompt in reply 及时回复
7. vivid and exact words 生动准确的话
8. minor mistake 小错误
9. above-mentioned 以上所提到的
10. lose out 输掉,失败

 Knowledge Consolidation 知识点巩固

我们和李娜一样,将来大多是国际贸易专业的从业人员,在张先生的指导下,我们学到了什么?是否掌握了书写商务信函的 7C 原则呢?我们的弱点在哪里?是否能将下面的内容进行归类呢?让我们一起来试试吧!

函电写作基本原则归类

一、(　　　　　　)

语言要有礼貌且谦虚,及时地回信也是礼貌的表现。

例如：

1) We have received with many thanks your letter of 20 May，and we take the pleasure of sending you our latest catalog. We wish to draw your attention to a special offer which we have made in it.

2) You will be particularly interested in a special offer on Page 5 of the latest catalog enclosed，which you requested in your letter of 20 May.

二、（　　　　）

写信时要处处从对方的角度去考虑具体的需求，而不是从自身出发，语气上要尊重对方。
例如：

1) You earn 2 percent discount when you pay cash. We will send you the brochure next month.

2) We allow 2 percent discount for cash payment. We won't be able to send you the brochure this month.

前者比后者要好很多。

三、（　　　　）

一封商业信函应概括各项必需的事项，如：邀请信应说明时间、地点等，切忌寄出表述含糊不清的信件。

四、（　　　　）

意思表达明确，要注意：

1. 避免用词错误

例如：As to the vessels sailing from Hong Kong to San Francisco，we have bimonthly direct services.

此处 bimonthly 有歧义：可以表示 twice a month，也可以是 once two months。故会使读信者感到迷惑，可以改写为：

1) We have two direct sailings every month from Hong Kong to San Francisco.

2) We have semimonthly（每半个月一次）direct sailing from Hong Kong to San Francisco.

3) We have a direct sailing once two months from Hong Kong to San Francisco.

2. 注意词语所放的位置

例如：

1) We shall be able to supply 10 cases of the item only.

2) We shall be able to supply 10 cases only of the item.

前者有两种以上商品的含义。

3. 注意句子的结构

例如：

1) Yesterday we sent you 5 samples of the goods which you requested in your letter of May 20 by air.

2）We sent you，by air，5 samples of the goods which you requested in your letter of May 20.

第二句的表达方式更为合理,因为将 by air 提前放到 sent 的后面强调了货是怎么发出的。所以这句话的中文意思是:你们 5 月 20 日的信件里所要求的产品,我们通过空运寄出了5 件样品。

而第一句则可以有另外一层意思:你们 5 月 20 日的航空信里所要求的产品,昨天我们寄出了 5 件样品。此处的 by air 是 letter 的后置定语。

五、（   ）

1. 避免废话连篇

例如：

1）"We wish to acknowledge receipt of your letter ..."可改为"We appreciate your letter ..."。

2）"Enclosed herewith please find two copies of ..."可改为"We enclose two copies of ..."。

2. 短句、单词的运用应避免不必要的重复

例如：

1）enclosed herewith→enclosed

2）at this time→now

3）due to the fact that→because

4）a draft in the amount of ＄1,000→a draft for ＄1,000

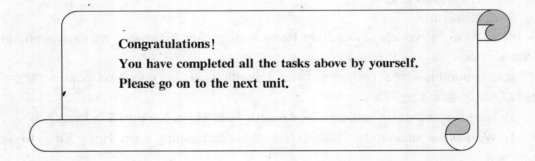

Congratulations!
You have completed all the tasks above by yourself.
Please go on to the next unit.

国际商务英语函电

Unit 2　Layout of a Business Letter

Situational Introduction 情景介绍

　　李娜已基本掌握了书写商务信函的 7C 原则,现在张先生要求她学习商务函电和信封的写作风格和格式。

Knowledge to Impart 知识传授

　　Mr. Zhang says that although there are different ways in business letter writing, people usually follow a certain standardized way in their business communication. Generally speaking, a well-constructed business letter should be made up of the seven **principal parts** detailed as follows:

　　1. Letterhead（信头）

　　2. Date（日期）

　　3. Inside Name & Address（封内地址）

　　4. Salutation（称呼）

　　5. Letter Body（信文）

　　6. Complimentary Close（结尾敬语）

　　7. Signature（签名）

　　(张先生说:尽管商务函电的写作方法不尽相同,但人们通常会在商务交流中遵循某一种规范的方法。一般来说,一封构思完美的商务信函都由以下七个主要部分组成,即:信头、日期、封内地址、称呼、信文、结尾敬语、签名)

　　Now Mr. Zhang is explaining these seven principal parts to Li Na.

1. Letterhead

Letterhead includes the essential particulars about the writer — the name of his company, the full address of the company, postcode, telephone number, fax number, Internet address and e-mail address. Usually it has been printed already. At present time, most of the big business companies use letterhead stationery for their letter communication. Sometimes a logo can be found in the letterhead, too.

Please look at this example:

 SHANGHAI ZHENGHUA SILK IMP./EXP. CORP.
6F, Youyou Yanqiao Mansion, 389 Pudian Rd.
Pudong New Area, Shanghai, China

2. Date

Date line is a vital part in a business letter. The date should always be written in a standard form. There are two ways in writing the date. You can write it in the logical order of day, month, year. For the day, either cardinal numbers or ordinal numbers can be used.

e. g. 17 June, 2012 or 17th June, 2012 (British way)

The day can also be written after the month. But a comma must be used between the day and the year.

e. g. July 18, 2012 (American way)

Please stay away from all-number form, for example, 6/5/2012. It may easily be confused, because in Britain the date means 6th May, 2012, but in the United States and some other countries it means 5th June, 2012. Remember the date line should be placed above the inside name and address.

3. Inside Name & Address

The inside address usually refers to the information about the receiver's. Generally, it includes all of the following information: the receiver's name and title, the company name, street address, city, state/province, ZIP code and the country. It is usually put one or two lines under the date line, at the top left-hand corner.

Here is an example:

Mr. George Allen
Personnel Manager
Shanghai Foreign Trade & Economics Training Center
78, Guizhou Rd., Huangpu District, Shanghai, 200002
P. R. China

国际商务英语函电

4. Salutation

The salutation is the polite greeting to begin a letter. On formal occasions or when you are not acquainted with the receiver, please use "Dear Sir" or "Dear Sirs", but "Gentlemen" is usually used instead of "Dear Sirs" by Americans or Canadians. If you know the readers' name, please write out his or her name as follows：（1）Dear Mr. Smith；（2）Dear Mrs. Brown；（3）Dear Miss Green；（4）Dear Ms. Sharp. Salutation is placed below the inside name and address.

5. Letter Body

It is the most important part of a letter. It contains the message you want to pass to your reader. Although you may find there are only a few words in a letter sometimes, you should still follow the three-paragraph format. The opening paragraph is the subject introduction of the letter. It should obtain the reader's attention at the first sight, and help to gain a positive response from the reader. The middle paragraph is the discussion of the deal in details. The last paragraph is as important as a summation, suggestion or further request. Furthermore, no matter the letter is short or long, you should follow the 7C's principles.

6. Complimentary Close

The complimentary close is a polite way to bring a letter to an end. The expression used must be suitable for the occasion and be in keeping with the salutation. For example, if the letter begins with "Dear Sir" or "Dear Madam", we usually use "Yours faithfully" or "Faithfully yours" as complimentary close; if the letter begins with "Dear Mr. James", "Dear Miss Walker" or other exact names, we should use "Yours sincerely" or "Sincerely yours" as complimentary close.

It is usually given from the second line below the closing sentence of the letter.

7. Signature

Signature is usually given three blank lines below the complimentary close. It usually consists of three lines like this：

（1）name of the writer's company
（2）manual signature of the writer（写信人的亲笔签名）
（3）typed name of the writer and his or her job title（写信人打印签名及工作职务）
e. g. China National Silk Imp. & Exp. Corp.

David Wang
David Wang（Manager of Import Dept.）

Li Na，an inquisitive girl，has got the general knowledge about seven **principal parts** of business letter writing. Now she is asking Mr. Zhang for some more related knowledge.

Let's learn together.

（李娜是一位勤学好问的小姑娘，她对商务信函书写的七个主要部分有了大致的了解，现在她请张先生给她讲讲更多的相关知识。我们一起来学学吧）

First let's look at Supplementary Elements（附加部分）.

★ Reference No.（发文编号）

It has three functions：first，it helps us to send them to the right person or department on time；second，it can provide our replies with good links to earlier correspondences；third，it enables us to find the needed one quickly. It is usually written below the letterhead.

 e.g. Your Ref. No. ALM/PS

   Our Ref. No. A1002

★ Attention Line（经办人栏）

Usually，when the receiver's name is not mentioned in the inside address，you should use the attention line to mention the individual's name to show whom the letter is really addressed to. The word "attention" or the phrase "for the attention" can be typed in capital way or underlined. It is usually placed on the second line below the inside address.

 e.g. ATTN：Mr. Francis Storm

★ Subject Line（标题）

The purpose of Subject Line is to draw attention to the topic of the letter. Usually it is centered over the body of the letter. We can plus "Re" before the Subject Line or not，meaning the reason of the letter.

 e.g. Your Order No. 5742

★ Enclosure（附件）

If a letter is accompanied by some other documents，you may indicate one or more enclosures，usually abbreviated.

 e.g. Enc. Price List

   Encls. 2 Invoices

If you have mentioned the enclosure already in the letter，you can use "a/s". Here "a/s" means "As stated".

 e.g. As stated（As above）附件：如文（如上）

★ Postscript（补充）

In a business letter，a postscript is usually not used in its original function. On the contrary，it serves as a device to emphasize something. It is usually used in the form of "P.S." below the enclosure. You should avoid using it，since it is always regarded as a sign of poor planning.

Now let's talk about the Format of a Business Letter.

There are different writing formats in business letters. The two most popular forms are the Full Blocked Format and the Semi-blocked Format. Please look at these two examples.

国际商务英语函电

Full Blocked Format 完全齐头式

SHANGHAI ZHENGHUA SILK IMP./EXP. CORP.
6F, Youyou Yanqiao Mansion, 389 Pudian Rd.
Pudong New Area, Shanghai, China

Your Ref. No. 121
Our Ref. No. A1002

17 May, 2012

EL Mar Trading Company
23 Richmond Street, Sheffield
U. K. S20 1BJ

ATTN: Mr. Francis Storm

Dear Sir,

Re: Your Order No. 5742

_____
_____
_____
_____
_____
_____

Yours faithfully,
Shanghai Zhenghua Silk Imp./Exp. Corp.
David Wang
David Wang (Manager of Import Dept.)

Encl. Price List

P.S.

国际商务英语函电

SHANGHAI ZHENGHUA SILK IMP. /EXP. CORP.
6F，Youyou Yanqiao Mansion，389 Pudian Rd.
Pudong New Area，Shanghai，China

Your Ref. No. 121
Our Ref. No. A1002

17 May，2012

EL Mar Trading Company
23 Richmond Street，Sheffield
U.K. S20 1BJ

ATTN：Mr. Francis Storm

Dear Sir，

Re：Your Order No. 5742

_____

_____
_____
_____
_____

Yours faithfully，
Shanghai Zhenghua Silk Imp. /Exp. Corp.
David Wang
David Wang（Manager of Import Dept.）

Encl. Price List

P. S.

Then let's talk about how to address an envelope. Here is the answer for you.

　　Accuracy, clearness and good appearance are the three important requirements in addressing an envelope. Generally speaking, the sender's address should be written in the upper left corner of the envelope, while the receiver's name and address should be written above half way down the envelope.

Here is an example：

SHANGHAI ZHENGHUA SILK IMP./EXP. CORP.
6F，Youyou Yanqiao Mansion，389 Pudian Rd.
Pudong New Area，Shanghai，China

EL Mar Trading Company
23 Richmond Street，Sheffield
U. K. S20 1BJ

STAMP

BY AIR MAIL
PAR AVION

What Mr. Zhang has explained is simple and easy to understand. Li Na has greatly appreciated his help. Now she would like to do some practice.

（张先生对知识点的讲解简单易懂，李娜十分感激他的帮助。现在她想进行一些操练）

Practice 小练习

Task 1：Answer the following questions.

1. What are the seven main parts that a business letter usually involves? Besides the seven parts，can you tell some other related knowledge?

　　_____

2. What are the two main formats of today's business letter? Which format do you think will be the most popular?

　　_____

3. What are the three important requirements in addressing an envelope?

　　_____

4. What does "P. S." stand for?

　　_____

5. What is the purpose of the subject line?

　　_____

6. Where is reference No. usually placed?

　　_____

国际商务英语函电

Task 2: Decide whether the following statements are true or false.

( ) 1. It is the same meaning of 2/6/2012 in British English and American English.

( ) 2. Nowadays, the block style (齐头式) is no longer used in business letters.

( ) 3. Usually, when the receiver's name is not mentioned in the inside address, you should use the attention line to mention the individual's name to show whom the letter is really addressed to.

( ) 4. In the letter body, the last paragraph is as important as a summation, suggestion or further request.

( ) 5. The complimentary close is a polite way of ending a letter.

( ) 6. The inside address is usually put one or two lines under the date line, aligned with the right margin(边沿).

( ) 7. The purpose of subject line is to draw attention to the topic of the letter.

( ) 8. In a very formal letter, if you don't have a close relation with the receiver, you can use his or her first name, such as "Dear Mary".

( ) 9. Date line is not important in a business letter, so you needn't write it in a standard form.

( ) 10. At present time, most of the big business companies use letterhead stationery for their letter communication.

Task 3: Choose the right answer for each sentence.

( ) 1. Letterhead is usually _____ on the top part of the letter.

A. placing   B. place   C. placed   D. places

( ) 2. Sometimes a logo can _____ in the letterhead in some business letters.

A. find   B. found   C. be finding   D. be found

( ) 3. Date line is a vital part in a business letter. Here "vital" means _____.

A. essential   B. living

C. dead   D. unimportant

( ) 4. The inside address usually refers to the information about the _____.

A. writer's   B. receiver's   C. sender's   D. postman's

( ) 5. In a very formal letter, you always need to address the reader with his surname. Here "address" means "_____".

A. speak seriously   B. make a formal speech

C. mark with a destination   D. call

( ) 6. _____ is the most important part of a formal letter.

A. Letter body   B. Letterhead

C. Complimentary close   D. Signature

( ) 7. In the letter body, the _____ paragraph is the subject introduction of the letter, which should obtain the reader's attention at the first sight.
   A. opening   B. middle   C. last   D. last but one

( ) 8. If you have mentioned the enclosure already in the body of a letter, you can use "a/s". Here "a/s" means "_____".
   A. about the state   B. as soon as possible
   C. all the staff   D. as stated

( ) 9. Date line such as "May 15, 2012" is of the _____ English style.
   A. British   B. American
   C. Australian   D. Irish

( ) 10. The subject line announces _____.
   A. whom the letter is written to
   B. where the letter is going
   C. what to do if the letter gets lost
   D. what the letter is about

 Comments & Suggestions 评价及建议

李娜成功完成了三项任务的操练,现在要求她熟记以下单词与词组。

1. particular [pə'tɪkjʊlə] *n*. 详细情况
2. postcode ['pəʊstˌkəʊd] *n*. 邮政编码
3. letterhead ['letəˌhed] *n*. 信头
4. communication [kəˌmjuːnɪ'keɪʃən] *n*. 通信,交往
5. logo ['ləʊgəʊ] *n*. 公司标志
6. stationery ['steɪʃənərɪ] *n*. 信纸,文具
7. vital ['vaɪtl] *a*. 重要的
8. logical ['lɒdʒɪkəl] *a*. 合理的,逻辑的
9. cardinal ['kɑːdɪnl] *a*. 基本的
10. ordinal ['ɔːdɪnəl] *a*. 顺序的

11. confuse [kən'fjuːz] *v*. 混淆,搞乱
12. comma ['kɒmə] *n*. 逗号
13. salutation [ˌsæljʊ'teɪʃən] *n*. 称呼
14. acquaint [ə'kweɪnt] *v*. 使了解,使熟悉
15. summation [sʌ'meɪʃən] *n*. 概括
16. complimentary [ˌkɒmplɪ'mentərɪ] *a*. 表示敬意的
17. signature ['sɪgnɪtʃə] *n*. 签名
18. align [ə'laɪn] *v*. 排列,对齐
19. silk [sɪlk] *n*. 丝绸,丝织物

• •

1. business communication   商务交流
2. principal part   主要部分
3. as follows   如下
4. standard form   标准形式
5. logical order   逻辑次序
6. cardinal number   基数

7. ordinal number　序数
8. ZIP code　邮政编码
9. be acquainted with ...　与……熟悉
10. positive response　肯定的答复
11. be in keeping with ...　与……保持一致

12. well-constructed　构思完美的
13. supplementary element　附加部分
14. full blocked format　完全齐头式
15. semi-blocked format　半齐头式或混合式
16. on the contrary　相反

Knowledge Consolidation 知识点巩固

　　在张先生的指导下,李娜掌握了商务函电和信封的写作风格和格式。我们是否有同样的收获呢? 下面我们一起来练练吧!

　　读下面的英语信函,根据信 A 中的内容以及所给回信 B 的中文内容完成 Task 1～4。

A

Upper Real Estate Co. Ltd.
1564 Montpelier Avenue
Oklahoma City, Oklahoma

May 23, 2012

Ecco. Inc.
1200 Mason Avenue
Paris, France

Dear Mr. /Ms. ,

Mr. John Green, our General Manager, will be in Paris from June 2 to 7 and would like to come and see you, say, on June 3 at 2:00 p. m. about the opening of a sample room there. Please let us know if the time is convenient for you. If not, what time you would suggest.

Yours faithfully,
Upper Real Estate Co. Ltd.
Jenny White
Jenny White (Secretary for GM)

B

内容:谢谢来函告知我方六月 2～7 日格林先生的来访。不巧,我们的总经理爱德华兹先

国际商务英语函电

生现正在开罗（Cairo），要到六月中旬才能回来。但他回来后愿意在任何时间会见格林先生。

落款：总经理助理 Sally Smith

_____ A _____

_____

_____ B _____

_____ C _____

_____

Dear _____ 1 _____ ,

    Thank you for your letter _____ 2 _____ of _____ 3 _____ during June 2 to 7. Unfortunately, Mr. Edwards, _____ 4 _____ is now _____ 5 _____ and _____ 6 _____ until _____ 7 _____. He would, however, be pleased to see Mr. Green _____ 8 _____.

    We _____ 9 _____ from you.

Yours faithfully，

_____ 10 _____

_____ 11 _____

Task 1：从方框中选出正确的内容填写信 B 中的空格 1～11。

> will not be back   Sally Smith   any time after his return   informing us
> look forward to hearing   Mr. Green's visit   the second half of June
> in Cairo   Assistant for GM   our manager   Ms. White

Task 2：根据来信内容在信 B 中填写空格 A～C。

Task 3：在信 A 中找出对应的项目并填写完整。

1. Letterhead：_____
2. Date：_____
3. Inside Address：_____
4. Salutation：_____
5. Complimentary Close：_____
6. Writer's Signature：_____

国际商务英语函电

Task 4: 请分别给信 A 和信 B 书写信封。

A

B

Congratulations!
You have completed all the tasks above by yourself.
Please go on to the next unit.

Unit 3　Establishing Business Relations

Situational Introduction 情景介绍

在张先生的指导下,李娜初步掌握了书写商务函电的基本要素:7C原则以及商务函电和信封的写作风格及格式。现在要求她学习书写与国外客户建立贸易关系的商务信函,我们一起来参与吧!

Knowledge to Impart 知识传授

No business transaction can be done without communication between business partners. A foreign trade company needs a worldwide business contact to keep and develop its business. Therefore, establishing business relations with prospective customers is the first important step in international trade.

(若贸易伙伴之间无沟通,交易是无法进行的。外贸公司要保持或扩大业务就需要广泛的洽商。因此,与潜在的客户建立业务关系是国际贸易中首要的一步)

Then how can we establish business relations with a new company or make ourselves known? Let's listen to Mr. Zhang's explanation !

(那么我们如何与一个新公司建立业务关系或是将自己介绍给别人呢? 让我们来听听张先生对此的解释吧)

1. Channels for Establishing Business Relations

In international business, the importer and the exporter are usually separated by thousands of miles. It's hard for them to find the real partners by themselves, so they can use the following channels to know each other.

a.　Recommendations from Banks（银行推荐）

Banks are always ready to provide the names and addresses of exporters in their respective cities.

b.　Chambers of Commerce in Foreign Countries（国外商会）

A chamber of commerce is an organization of businessmen. One of its tasks is to get business information and to find new opportunities for its members.

c.　Commercial Counselor's Office（商务参赞处）

Necessary information can be obtained from the commercial counselor's office.

d. Newspaper or Online Ads（报纸或广告）

Another way to get the information you want is to read newspapers or online ads.

e. Trade Fairs and Exhibitions（交易会和展会）

Attending trade fairs and exhibitions held both at home and abroad will also supply many new contacts, introduction and general information.

f. Mutual Visits by Trade Delegations and Groups（贸易代表团和小组进行互访）

This will help to enhance the communication of different business markets, attract investment interest and obtain more future business opportunities.

g. Introduce Yourself on the Internet or Be Introduced by Your Friends（互联网上自我介绍或通过朋友介绍）

It is a good way to get new contacts, discover potential business opportunities and make a reputation of yourself in industry.

> **Tips**
>
> After obtaining the name and address of your potential trade partner, you can contact him or her to establish business relations. But before starting a concrete transaction, you should make the necessary status investigation concerning the financial position, credit, reputation, and business methods of your future business partner.
>
> （在获得潜在客户的姓名、地址后,你可以与之取得联系并建立业务关系。但在开始进行一笔具体的交易之前,你应该做些必要的资信调查,即对对方公司的财务状况、信用、声誉及业务做法等情况进行了解）

2. Request for Establishing Business Relations

请阅读以下请求建立业务关系的商务信函并将它译成中文。

Dear Sir/Madam,

We have known your name and address from the East-China Fair（华东交易会）and we are pleased to find that your goods can meet our demands, so we are writing to you in the hope of establishing business relations with you.

Our company is located in Pudong New Area, Shanghai City. And we are one of the leading importers of silk piece goods and products in Shanghai and well-connected with all the major wholesalers and retailers. Therefore, we are sure that we can sell large quantities of your goods if you can make us offers at a competitive price.

It would be appreciated if you can send us a copy of your latest catalog together with your price.

We are looking forward to receiving your early reply.

Yours faithfully,
George Allen
Sales Manager

3. Promoting Business Relationship

这是上海中轩实业有限公司写给澳大利亚悉尼全球有限公司的一封求购信函,请认真阅读并注意此信的格式。

SHANGHAI SINODOOR INDUSTRY CO. LTD.
Room 102，No.64，Lane 1800，Dong Fang Rd.
Pudong New Area，Shanghai，P.R. China

May 28，2012

Global Co. Ltd.
87 Flint Street
Sydney，Australia

Dear Sir/Madam，

Re：Embroidered Table-cloths

We learn from the First Commercial Bank at your end that your firm specializes in the manufacture and export of textiles，and would like to take this opportunity to enter into business relationship with you. Now we are in the market for Embroidered Table-cloths from your company.

If you can assure us of a competitive price，excellent quality and prompt delivery，we shall be able to place an order for these goods on a substantial scale. We，therefore，ask you to furnish us with a full range of samples，assorted colors together with your lowest quotations and the related terms and conditions.

As to our credit standing，you may approach the following bank：

国际商务英语函电

Industrial and Commercial Bank of China, Shanghai Branch

We are looking forward with keen interest to hearing from you.

Yours faithfully,
Wang Ling
Assistant Manager

4. Replying to the Promoting Business Relationship

这是来自澳大利亚悉尼全球有限公司的复函,请认真阅读并说说此信的写作风格与前一封信的风格有什么区别。

Global Co. Ltd.
87 Flint Street
Sydney, Australia

June 2, 2012

SHANGHAI SINODOOR INDUSTRY CO. LTD.
Room 102, No. 64, Lane 1800, Dong Fang Rd.
Pudong New Area, Shanghai, P. R. China

ATTN: Miss Wang Ling

Dear Sir/Madam,

Many thanks for your letter of May 28, 2012. We are very pleased to send you separately the samples of Embroidered Table-cloths together with the respective price list.

Please note that Item No. 34B and No. 45T can be certainly promised for prompt shipment upon receipt of your order, subject to the establishing of an irrevocable and confirmed letter of credit for the corresponding amount of order, valid for a period of 60 days.

We wish to draw your attention to the fact that the increasing cost of raw materials for these articles will make us raise their selling prices, and that the present prices can no longer be guaranteed, if your orders are not placed forthwith.

国际商务英语函电

We trust that your initial order will be placed with us without delay.

Yours faithfully,
Global Co. Ltd.
Paul Johnson
Manager

Encl. Price Lists

What Mr. Zhang has explained is easy to understand. He not only gives Li Na new knowledge，but also helps her review what she has learned before. We have learned a lot just like Li Na. Now let's do some practice with her.

（张先生的讲解简单易懂，他不仅教授给李娜新的知识，还对前面所学的知识进行了回顾，我们跟李娜一样受益匪浅。现在我们和李娜一起进行操练吧）

 Practice 小练习

Task 1：Answer the following questions.

1. Can business transaction be completed without communication between business partners?

   _____

2. Does a foreign trade company need a worldwide business contact to keep and develop its business?

   _____

3. To establish business relations with prospective customers is the first important step in international trade，isn't it?

   _____

4. How can the importer and the exporter establish business relations with each other or make themselves known as both of them are usually separated by thousands of miles? Please give some examples.

   _____

   _____

Task 2：Decide whether the following statements are true or false.

（   ）1. Business transaction can be done without communication between business partners.

（   ）2. In international trade，the first important step is to establish business relations with prospective customers.

国际商务英语函电

(   ) 3. If a foreign trade company desires to keep and develop its business, it needs a worldwide business contact with his business partners.

(   ) 4. In foreign trade, the importer and the exporter are usually separated by thousands of miles, so it's not easy for them to find the real partners by themselves.

(   ) 5. In world trade, if we like to establish business relations with a new company, the following channels can help us:

a. Recommendations from banks;

b. Chambers of Commerce in foreign countries;

c. Commercial counselor's office;

d. Newspapers or online ads;

e. Trade fairs and exhibitions;

f. Mutual visits by trade delegations and groups;

g. Introduce yourself on the Internet or be introduced by your friends.

Task 3: Choose the right answer for each sentence.

(   ) 1. Your name and address _____ to us by your Chambers of Commerce.

A. was given　　　　　　　　　B. have given

C. were give　　　　　　　　　D. have been given

(   ) 2. We are very glad to enter _____ business relations _____ your company.

A. into ... with　　　　　　　B. with ... into

C. into ... for　　　　　　　　D. with ... in

(   ) 3. We shall send you the samples _____ receipt of your inquiries.

A. to　　　　B. upon　　　　C. with　　　　D. for

(   ) 4. Our firm is specialized _____ the manufacture and export of textiles.

A. at　　　　B. in　　　　C. on　　　　D. /

(   ) 5. We assure our clients _____ the best service _____ any time.

A. with ... at　　　　　　　　B. of ... at

C. in... in　　　　　　　　　D. about... at

(   ) 6. They are _____ Embroidered Table-cloths from your company.

A. in the market for　　　　　B. at the market for

C. on the market with　　　　D. at market for

(   ) 7. We expect these practices to cease <u>forthwith</u>. The underlined word means _____.

A. at once　　　　　　　　　B. short

C. very　　　　　　　　　　　D. immediate

国际商务英语函电

( ) 8. This contract is _____ three years.
   A. valid   B. valid at   C. valid with   D. valid for
( ) 9. We _____ delivery _____ two weeks.
   A. guarantees … with   B. guarantees … within
   C. guarantee … within   D. guarantee … after
( ) 10. We have received your letter of May 28，2012 _____ we thank you.
   A. for that   B. for what
   C. for which   D. with which
( ) 11. We hope this unfortunate incident will not affect the friendly relations _____ us.
   A. on   B. between   C. in   D. for
( ) 12. We are glad that in the past few years，_____ our joint efforts（共同努力），we have greatly promoted both business and friendship.
   A. through   B. with   C. by   D. at

Comments & Suggestions 评价及建议

李娜出色地完成了三项任务，现在要求她熟练掌握以下单词与词组。

1. initial [ɪˈnɪʃəl] a. 开始的，初次的
2. status [ˈsteɪtəs] n. 情况，状况
3. prospective [prəˈspektɪv] a. 未来的
4. counselor [ˈkaʊnsələ] n. 顾问，参事
5. commercial [kəˈmɜːʃəl] a. 商业的，商务的
6. delegation [ˌdelɪˈɡeɪʃən] n. 代表团
7. investigation [ɪnˌvestɪˈɡeɪʃən] n. 调查，研究
8. financial [faɪˈnænʃəl] a. 财政的，金融的
9. reputation [ˌrepjʊˈteɪʃən] n. 名誉，名声
10. quotation [kwəʊˈteɪʃən] n. 报价，引用
11. appreciate [əˈpriːʃɪeɪt] v. 欣赏，

感激
12. furnish [ˈfɜːnɪʃ] v. 供应，提供
13. substantial [səbˈstænʃəl] a. 大量的，丰盛的
14. embroider [ɪmˈbrɔɪdə] v. 绣（花纹）（+on）
15. assorted [əˈsɔːtɪd] a. 各种各样，合适的
16. approach [əˈprəʊtʃ] v. 接近，与……联系
17. separately [ˈsepərɪtlɪ] adv. 各自地，分别地
18. forthwith [ˈfɔːθˈwɪð] adv. 立刻，马上
19. irrevocable [ɪˈrevəkəbl] a. 不可撤销的
20. potential [pəˈtenʃəl] a. 潜在的，可能的

21. guarantee [ˌɡærən'tiː] *n*. 保证书 *v*. 担保

22. corresponding [ˌkɒrɪ'spɒndɪŋ] *a*. 一致的

23. transaction [træn'zækʃən] *n*. 交易，买卖

24. recommendation [ˌrekəmen'deɪʃən] *n*. 推荐

25. catalog ['kætəlɒɡ] *n*. 产品目录

● ●

1. prospective customer 潜在客户
2. first important step 首要的一步
3. Chambers of Commerce in foreign countries 国外商会
4. Commercial Counselor's Office 商务参赞处
5. trade fair 交易会
6. mutual visits 互访
7. establish business relations 建立贸易关系
8. status investigation 资信调查
9. financial position 财务状况
10. East-China Fair 华东交易会
11. specialize in 专门经营
12. be in the market for 要买(货物)
13. at *sb*.'s end 在某人处
14. upon receipt of *sth*. 一收到某物，就……
15. embroidered table-cloth 绣花台布
16. lowest quotation 最低报价
17. credit standing 信用状况
18. on a substantial scale 批量
19. assorted colors 各种各样的颜色
20. respective price list 各自的价目表
21. leading importers 主要进口商

 Knowledge Consolidation 知识点巩固

在张先生的带教下，李娜学到了很多，现在她已经知道如何与国外公司建立贸易关系，怎样写好往来信函了。然而，我们在书写商务信函时，会用到很多关键的词语，这些词语常常是一词多义，在不同的情形会有不同的含义。现在我们以本单元的相关词语为例，来学学它们的精彩之处吧！

1. appreciate *vt*. 感激，理解，欣赏

e.g. （1）Those foreign businessmen highly appreciate（欣赏）the Chinese arts and crafts.

（2）We hope that you will appreciate（理解）our position. This is our lowest price and we can't reduce it further.

（3）Your early reply will be highly appreciated（感激）.

（4）Her talent for music was not appreciated. 她的音乐才能无人赏识。

appreciate doing *sth*. 对……很感激

e.g. We shall appreciate receiving your further orders. 如下更多的订单，不胜感谢。

It will be appreciated if ... 如果……我们将非常感谢。

e.g. It will be appreciated if you will understand our difficulties.

appreciate *vi.*（土地、货币等）增值（＋in）

e. g. Land will continue to appreciate. 土地将继续增值。

2. upon/on/after receipt of *sth*. 一收到某物,就……

c. f.（比较） in receipt of 表示收到的状态

e. g. （1）Upon receipt of your L/C, we will make shipment without delay.

（2）We are in receipt of your L/C dated Feb. 28th, from which we've known that you hope to enter into trade relations with us.

3. make *sb*. an offer（for *sth*.） 向某人报盘

offers 可分为 firm offers（实盘）与 non-firm offers（虚盘）,也可分别表达为 offers with engagement 与 offers without engagement。

向某人报出某物的实盘：make *sb*. a firm offer for *sth*.

e. g. If your order is large enough, we can make you a firm offer for Shandong Groundnuts at a competitive price.

4. be well connected with 与某人关系很好

e. g. He is a cheerful person and well connected with his workmates.

5. wholesalers and retailers 批发商和零售商

c. f. wholesale trade and retail trade 批发贸易和零售贸易

wholesale price and retail price 批发价和零售价

6. latest catalog and price list 最新的商品目录册及价格表

latest 这里指最晚印刷,距现在最近的意思。

e. g. latest market report 最新市场报告

latest entry 最新（输入的）记录

7. establish business relations with *sb*. ＝ enter into business relations with *sb*. 建立贸易关系

8. Commercial Counselor's Office 商务参赞处（一般设在各国的驻外使馆内）

counselor *n*. ① 顾问,参事 ②（协助学生解决问题的）指导老师

9. assorted *a*. ① 各色的,什锦的；各种各样（混在一起）的

②（常构成复合词）相配的,合适的

e. g. （1）Mom bought a box of assorted chocolates. 妈妈买了一盒什锦巧克力。

（2）Anne and David are an ill-assorted pair. 安妮和戴维是不相配的一对。

assorted colors 各种各样的颜色

e. g. In order to facilitate (promote) selling, it will be better to pack the goods with equally assorted colors. 为了便于销售,最好将货物各种颜色平均搭配装箱。

10. embroider *v.* ① 绣(花纹)(＋on) ② 在(织物)上绣花纹(＋with)

e. g. (1) I embroidered wild flowers on this pillow. 我在这枕头上绣了野花。

(2) She embroidered a tablecloth for me. 她为我绣了块桌布。

(3) The shirt was embroidered with some birds. 这衬衣上绣了一些鸟。

11. furnish *sb.* **with** *sth.* = supply *sb.* with *sth.*; provide *sb.* with *sth.* 将某物提供给某人

12. East-China Fair 华东交易会(简称华交会)

c. f. The China Export Commodity Fair/the Guangzhou Fair/the Canton Fair 中国出口商品交易会(简称广交会)

13. with keen interest 殷切地

e. g. We trust the above offer will be acceptable to you and await your trial order with keen interest. 我们相信,上述报盘贵方是可以接受的,热切期待贵方的试单。

14. specialize in/to be specialized in 专门经营

c. f. handle *vt.* 经营,经办,搬运

deal/trade in *sth.* 从事某物交易

in the line of *sth.* 从事某一行业,经营某一产品

e. g. (1) Many girl students specialize in medicine. 许多女学生专攻医科。

(2) They have handled import and export for many years. 该公司已多年做进出口生意。

(3) We deal in electronic products. 我们经营电子产品。

(4) We are in the line of textiles. 我们经营纺织品。

15. in the market for ＝wish to buy or want to buy 要买(货物)

e. g. They are in the market for Haier brand washing machines. 他们想购买海尔洗衣机。

c. f. in the market 要买或要卖

e. g. (1) Please send us your orders when you are again in the market. 当贵方再购买时,请发订单。

(2) Please quote us your lowest price when you are again in the market. 当贵方想再卖时,请报最低价。

Task 1: Fill in the blanks with the words and phrases given.

financial standing	on the basis of	in the line of	in the market for
workable	be specialized in	be interested in	in the hope of
approach	reputation	appreciate	recommend

国际商务英语函电

1. At present，we are _____ various kinds of Chinese arts and crafts and would _____ receiving your catalog and quotations.

2. We have been _____ arts and crafts for many years.

3. We wish to introduce ourselves to you as a professional company which _____ ____ all kinds of women's garments and _____ setting up mutually beneficial business relations with your firm.

4. As to our _____ , we wish to refer you to our bank in London.

5. We are willing to establish business relations with your firm _____ equality and mutual benefit.

6. We have come to known your name and address from the ABC Company，New York and take pleasure of writing to you _____ entering into business relations with you.

7. They are enjoying an excellent _____ .

8. Your firm has been _____ to us by the Chambers of Commerce in Tokyo，Japan.

9. They shall _____ the department concerned on this matter.

10. If your prices are _____ , we trust considerable business can materialize （实现）.

Task 2：Translation work.

A. Please put the following into Chinese.

Dear Sir/Madam，

Through the courtesy of （承蒙……引荐） the Commercial Counselor's Office of your Embassy in China，we learn that your firm is interested in establishing business relations with a Chinese firm to sell chemical products.

As one of the largest importers，we have been engaged in this line for many years and are connected with all the major dealers here. Therefore，we feel sure that we can sell large quantities of your goods if your offers are favorable. We would like you to send us a catalog and price list，and possibly some samples of the goods that you are principally interested in selling，so that we can study the sales possibility in our market.

As to our credit standing, please refer to Bank of China, Beijing.

We look forward to the pleasure of hearing from you.

Yours faithfully,

×××

B. Please put the following into English.

Dear Sir/Madam,

我们乐意向您自荐,作为一家国有企业(state-owned enterprise),我们从事罐头食品出口业务,期望与贵公司建立业务关系。

我们是中国最大的罐头食品制造商及出口商,去年我们的罐头食品出口共计10亿美金,占全国总量的30%(accounting for 30% of the national total)。

为使贵方对我们的产品有一个概括的了解,现随函寄上我公司经营产品的小册子一套,内有详细的有关产品规格及包装的说明。

若蒙早复,不胜感谢。

(结尾敬语:Yours faithfully)

Congratulations!
You have completed all the tasks above by yourself.
Please go on to the next unit.

Unit 4　Enquiries and Replies

Situational Introduction 情景介绍

　　周一上午,李娜发现她的桌上放着一封待处理的传真信件,是发给他们出口部的,但信的内容和形式她是第一次看到,因此她产生了很多疑惑。于是她兴冲冲地来到她的带教老师张先生的办公室请教。张先生正在接听客户的电话,示意她在一旁坐下。打完电话后,张先生亲切地问李娜有什么事,于是李娜把这封信函交给了张先生。

May 19，2012

Dear Sirs，

We are pleased to inform you that we have now enlarged our kitchen utensil department and are considering the addition of new products.

Your various electronic ovens would fit in well. Please send a complete range of catalogs and samples that are in production. We expect you to quote your lowest prices and would like to know whether you can supply from stock.

If we decide to put your goods into the market，we want your assurance that you will not sell them to other firms in this region.

We look forward to your early reply.

Yours faithfully，
Peter Pan

Knowledge to Impart 知识传授

Mr. Zhang: Li Na，this is an enquiry letter and it brings the opportunity of business to our organization. An enquiry is generally a request from an importer to an exporter to invite a quotation and/or an offer for the goods he wishes to buy or simply asking for some

国际商务英语函电

general information about these goods.

（李娜，这是一封询盘，它会给我们企业带来商机。询盘通常是进口商写给出口商的一封信，其目的是为了得到对方就有关商品的报价或只是想了解对方出口商品的信息）

There are two kinds of enquiry letters. One is called **General Enquiry** and the other is called **Specific Enquiry**. A General Enquiry is an enquiry written to get some general ideas about the products the buyer is interested in. Under this circumstance，the buyer asks the seller to send him or her catalogs，price lists and samples. A Specific Enquiry is written to get some more detailed information about the products the buyer wants to buy right away.

（询盘分为两种：一般性询盘和具体性询盘。一般性询盘只是获得关于买方感兴趣的商品的初步信息。在这种情况下，买方会要求卖方寄发产品目录、价格表和样品。具体性询盘则是直接询问买方有意购买的商品的细节）

Li Na： OK，I see. So it is a **General Enquiry**，isn't it?

Mr. Zhang： Exactly.

Li Na： What do we need to pay attention to while writing an enquiry letter?

Mr. Zhang： It is a very good question，Li Na. Here are some points to **keep in mind：**

1. Enquiries mean potential business. Prompt and careful replies are of great importance.（询盘意味着商机，及时和谨慎回复是至关重要的）

2. When making enquiries，give details of your own firm and ask for needed information from your prospective supplier. Be specific and state exactly what you want：the goods specification, a catalog, a sample, a quotation, etc.，so as to enable the seller to quote or offer the correct goods.（当你书写一封询盘时，应该提供本公司的具体情况并就需要了解的信息向供应方提出询问。必须做到具体并表明你意图了解的诸如产品规格、商品目录、样品和报价等，这样卖方才可以提供并报相关产品的价格）

Li Na： Thank you very much，Mr. Zhang.

Mr. Zhang： You are welcome. Here I have got some exercises concerning Enquiry for you to complete by tomorrow，do you want to have a try?

Li Na： OK，I will try my best.

李娜回家认真地进行练习，我们也来试一下吧！

 Practice 小练习

Task 1：Read through the dialog between *Robert* and *Kathy*，and fill in the blanks using the words and expressions given in the box below.

idea	negotiate	discount
in	consider	attractive

国际商务英语函电

Robert: Could you give us some _____1_____ about your prices?

Kathy: OK. Here are our latest price sheets. You'll see that our price is very _____2_____.

Robert: May I ask if you allow any _____3_____?

Kathy: Please tell me what you have _____4_____ mind.

Robert: From European suppliers we usually get a 5 percent discount, and sometimes 10 percent.

Kathy: If your order is large enough, we'll _____5_____ giving you some discount.

Robert: Fine! We'll _____6_____ after we decide how many machine tools we are going to order from you.

Task 2: Choose the best answer to complete each of the following sentences.

(   ) 1. Will you let us know how long _____ will take to deliver the goods?

    A. that   B. it   C. this

(   ) 2. We have an enquiry _____ large quantities of chemical fertilizer.

    A. at   B. for   C. in

(   ) 3. Your enquiry is having our prompt _____ and we hope to make you an offer in a few days.

    A. attention   B. settlement   C. arrangement

(   ) 4. We trust our offer will be _____ to you and await your order.

    A. accepted   B. accepting   C. acceptable

(   ) 5. The buyer _____ whom we have discussed the business offers for both rice and wheat wrote again today.

    A. with   B. to   C. of

(   ) 6. _____ to your letter enquiring for our TV sets, we have forwarded your enquiry for the attention of the biggest TV company.

    A. Refer   B. Referring   C. Referred

(   ) 7. We shall be pleased to supply you _____ any information you may require on this matter.

    A. of   B. to   C. with

(   ) 8. When an importer intends to make purchases of some goods, he sends a letter of _____ to an exporter.

    A. quotation   B. offer   C. enquiry

Task 3: Fill in the blanks with proper words.

1. Many clients are enquiring _____ our products.

2. Please quote us the best price _____ 50 sets of sewing machine.

国际商务英语函电

3. We prefer Red Leaf brand _____ Swallow brand.

4. Please send us your price list _____ your new items.

5. It would be _____ if samples can be sent to us.

6. Could you quote us your lowest price, CIF Vancouver, _____ 5% commission.

Task 4: Translate the following sentences into Chinese.

1. From your trade office here, we know you are a manufacturer of car components and are interested in distributing your products in our local market.

_____

2. We are interested in your electronic products and hope to receive your latest catalog and price list soon.

_____

3. We are looking for the hand tools and please advise if you are able to supply this item.

_____

Li Na has completed all the tasks. Next morning, she goes to Mr. Zhang's office to learn more about the enquiry letter.

Li Na: Mr. Zhang, could you tell me how to reply this kind of enquiry letter?

Mr. Zhang: No problem. Reply letters answer questions, supply information and/or materials, offer special help and attempt to satisfy the needs of those who make the requests. When giving replies to enquiries, make sure that you have answered all the customer's questions, include all the points you want to make, and assure your customer that you have faith in your product or service, which means that you have to "sell" it.

（回复函需要回答对方的问题,提供信息和/或有关材料,提供具体的帮助并尽力满足对方的要求。当回复询盘的时候,必须确保回答客户所有的询问并充分表达你的观点,力求让客户感受到你对自己产品或服务的信心,也就是说你需要"推销"产品）

Li Na: I see, but can you give me some tips on writing reply letters?

Mr. Zhang: Sure. First it is better practice to reply the customer's enquiry as soon as possible, maybe on the same day or the next day to show courtesy and efficiency. Secondly the questions in the enquiry letter should be answered properly and you should promise to answer the rest questions if you are sure of some of the questions. Last but not least it is a tactic to take this opportunity to promote your products or service.

（首先,收到客户询盘后,最好当天或隔天马上回复,以示礼貌及效率。其次,书写回复函只要针对客户的询问一一作答,如果其中有一两项问题无法马上回复,也要记得在回函中

告知对方可以回答的预计时间。最后，在回复的同时，也要利用一点推销技巧，突出本公司产品的品质和服务质量）

Here let's have a look at an example of reply letter.

Reply to a General Enquiry

May 15th，2012

Dear Sirs，

We are pleased to learn from your enquiry of April 20 that you like our range of silk blouses. We are in a position to supply you from our wide selection of shirts and blouses which we make for all age groups. We can offer you the quantity discount of 3% if you ask for orders over US $40,000. We usually accept confirmed，irrevocable letters of credit payable by draft at sight.

Enclosed you will find our summer catalog and price list. We are sure you will find a ready sale for our products in the U.S.A. as they have been sold well throughout Asia and Europe. Any orders you may place with us will receive our prompt attention.

Yours faithfully，
Robert Black

I can also offer you some useful sentence patterns and structures of a reply letter.

1. We **thank** you **for** your enquiry of June 18. As requested，we enclose a catalog and a price list for your perusal.
2. **Thanks for** your enquiry dated August 21. We are sending you our complete catalog，in which you will find a full description of our entire line of goods.
3. **In reply to** your enquiry of September 17，we are sending you by separate post a catalog and a sample book for your reference.
4. **We are glad to learn** from your enquiry of Feb. 8th that you are interested in our ladies' blouses. As requested，our catalog and price list are enclosed together with details of our sale conditions.

Li Na：Thank you so much.
Mr. Zhang：It is all right. Now it is time for you to do some practice.

国际商务英语函电

Knowledge Consolidation 知识点巩固

Task 1: Fill in the blanks in the reply letter written by Li Na.

Reply Letter

May 20, 2012

Dear Sirs,

We are pleased to learn _____1_____ your enquiry of May 19 that you like our range of kitchen utensils.

We are in a position to _____2_____ you from stock our wide selection of electronic ovens. We can offer you the quantity discount of 3% if you ask for an order of US $ 5,000. Up till _____3_____ we have no agents or representatives in your area and you will be our sole customer there. We usually accept confirmed, irrevocable letters of credit payable by draft at sight.

_____4_____ you will find our summer catalog and price list quoting prices CFR C3% New York. We are sure you will find a ready sale for our products in East Asia as they have been sold well throughout other regions of Asia. Any orders you may place with us will have our prompt attention.

Yours faithfully,
Li Na

Task 2: Choose the best answer to complete each of the following sentences.

(　　) 1. We _____ you _____ our E-mail of August 18th.
　　　　　A. send ... in　　　　　　　　　B. refer ... in
　　　　　C. give ... to　　　　　　　　　D. refer ... to

(　　) 2. Please let us have the details of your Panda brand color TV sets, _____ us your earliest delivery.
　　　　　A. give　　　　B. to give　　　　C. giving　　　　D. given

(　　) 3. We await _____ from you.
　　　　　A. hear　　　　B. hearing　　　　C. to hear　　　　D. to hearing

(　　) 4. We'd like to take this _____ to introduce ourselves as one of the leading importers in our country.
　　　　　A. chance　　　　B. time　　　　C. occasion　　　　D. opportunity

( ) 5. We have _____ the Oceania Trading Co. _____ the supply of radios.
      A. approached with … in   B. got in touch with … for
      C. approached … for   D. contacted with … for

( ) 6. We shall appreciate _____ us CIF Melbourne.
      A. you quote   B. you to quote
      C. your quoting   D. to you quoting

Task 3: Supply the missing words in the blanks and translate the letter into Chinese.

Dear Sirs,

We t_____ you for your e_____ of November
22. Under c_____ , you will f_____ a brochure
giving details i_____ about our Flying Tiger brand
motor-boats and i_____ the good results we h____
____ achieved in tests.

As regards trade d_____ , we will a_____ you
8% off list p_____ , with q_____ discount of
5% for o_____ over US $20,000.

Please don't hesitate to c_____ us if we can be of
any f_____ help to y_____ .

Yours faithfully,
×××

Task 4: Translate the Chinese parts into English.

1. If you are interested, _____（请即来电）.

2. As the price quoted by us is reasonable, _____
   ____（我们相信这将是你们所能接受的）.

3. We wish to advise that _____（样品及商品目录已另
   邮寄去）.

4. _____（如果你方不能供应一等品），we will take the
   second grade.

5. We shall appreciate it _____（如果你方给我方200辆
   自行车的报价）.

6. We shall be grateful _____（如果你方能寄来有关你
   方市场情况的报告）.

Comments & Suggestions 评价及建议

李娜出色地完成了四项任务，现在要求她熟练掌握以下单词与词组。

1. inform [ɪn'fɔːm] v. 通知
2. enlarge [ɪn'lɑːdʒ] v. 扩大
3. addition [ə'dɪʃən] n. 增加
4. various ['veərɪəs] a. 各种各样的
5. sample ['sæmpl] n. 样品
6. quote [kwəut] v. 报价
7. assurance [ə'ʃuərəns] n. 保证
8. region ['riːdʒən] n. 地区
9. request [rɪ'kwest] v. & n. 要求
10. prompt [prɒmpt] a. 及时的
11. discount ['dɪskaunt] n. 折扣
12. advise [əd'vaɪz] v. 告知
13. tip [tɪp] n. 建议
14. promote [prə'məut] v. 促进
15. blouse [blauz] n. 女式衬衫
16. perusal [pə'ruːzl] n. 细读
17. utensil [juː'tensl] n. 器具，用具；器皿；家庭厨房用具
18. range [reɪndʒ] n. 范围；射程；类别
19. draft [drɑːft] n. 汇票

20. enclosed [ɪn'kləuzd] a. 被附上的
21. negotiate [nɪ'gəuʃɪeɪt] v. 谈判，协商，交涉
22. deliver [dɪ'lɪvə] v. 发表；递送；交付
23. settlement ['setlmənt] n. 解决；结算
24. trust [trʌst] n. & v. 相信，信任
25. refer [rɪ'fɜː] v. 提到；针对；关系到；请教
26. intend [ɪn'tend] v. 意欲，计划
27. commission [kə'mɪʃən] n. 佣金，手续费
28. delivery [dɪ'lɪvərɪ] n. 传送，投递；（正式）交付
29. occasion [ə'keɪʒən] n. 机会，时机；场合
30. regard [rɪ'gɑːd] n. & v. 关系；注意
31. trade [treɪd] v. & n. 贸易；行业；买卖
32. hesitate ['hezɪteɪt] v. 犹豫，踌躇

• •

1. fit in   适合
2. supply from stock   现货供应
3. put ... into market   投放市场
4. right away   立即
5. of great importance   非常重要
6. attempt to   试图
7. have faith in   有信心
8. at sight   即期
9. chemical fertilizer   化工肥料

　　李娜利用休息时间查找了询盘和回复函的基本内容，以及一些相关句型，以备将来使用，整理如下：

I.　How to write letters of enquiry.

1	Introducing your firm and the products it deals in to the reader: We are ...
2	Stating the purpose of your letter: We are seeking a supplier of ...
3	Including a description or specification of the goods you require: A full specification of our requirements is given on the attached sheet.
4	Explaining what you want the recipient to do: Please quote us your best price and shipping date.
5	Stating your terms and methods of payment: We usually pay by confirmed 60-day irrevocable letter of credit.
6	Ending on an optimistic note and request an early reply: We hope to be able to place future orders with you if ...

II. How to write replies to letters of enquiry.

1	Express your thanks for the enquiry and state the date of the letter you received.
2	Supply all the information one enquired and inform that the catalogs, the price lists, samples and all the buyers requested have been sent by separate cover.
3	Offer detailed information about the products you can supply and the advantages of the products. Introduce something more about your company, which are the advantages of doing business with each other.
4	State that the price given is reasonable and competitive.
5	State terms of payment you can receive and the possible time for delivery.
6	End with a closing sentence of hope that the reader will be satisfied with your products and the hope to conduct business in the future.

III. Useful sentence patterns and substitutions.

1. We visited your stand at the

> Guangzhou Fair
> Paris Trade Exhibition
> World Expo 2010
> New York World's Fair

and are now writing to you

to enquire about your products.

2. Please

> send
> forward
> submit
> dispatch

your illustrated catalogs and mail the latest price list to us at

your earliest convenience.

国际商务英语函电

3. Perhaps at the same time you could quote us your

lowest
keenest
prevailing
competitive

prices for the said

commodities.

4. We would also like to know your

terms of payment.
terms of business.
terms and conditions.
discount terms.
trade terms.

5. We are

enclosing
mailing/sending to you
attaching to this letter
submitting to you by airmail
dispatching you by EMS

our illustrated catalog and export prices.

Congratulations!
You have completed all the tasks above by yourself.
Please go on to the next unit.

Unit 5 Offers and Counter-offers

Situational Introduction 情景介绍

　　李娜今天的工作是就海外客户的询问信发一份发盘。虽然在上周她已学习了回复询盘（reply to enquiry）的基本知识和句型，但撰写一份正式的、具有法律效力的发盘还是要求很高的，对她来说有点棘手。于是她带着一些问题请教她的带教老师张先生。

Knowledge to Impart 知识传授

Li Na：Sorry to bother you，Mr. Zhang，but are you free now?

Mr. Zhang：Yes，I'm available at the moment.

Li Na：It's very kind of you. I received an enquiry email from a Canadian buyer who showed great interest in our product. I am so glad that I can make the first offer in my working life.

Mr. Zhang：Good news. One party of the transaction，in order to sell or buy an item of goods，put forward some terms and conditions relevant to the transaction，expressing a willingness to make a deal. This is called an offer.

　　（交易的一方为了销售或购买一批商品，向另一方提出有关的交易条件，并表示愿按这些条件达成一笔交易，称作发盘）

　　A **counteroffer** is an expression for disagreement with the content of the offer，making amendment or addition or limitation to it.

　　（还盘是指受盘人对发盘内容不完全同意而提出修改或变更的表示，是对发盘条件进行添加、限制或其他更改的答复）

Li Na：I've written an offer letter，would you please check it for me?

Mr. Zhang：OK. Four essential elements must be contained in an offer letter：details of prices；discounts and terms of payments；date of delivery；the period of validity.

　　（在一封发盘信中必须包含四个基本要素：价格、折扣和付款方式、装运期和发盘的有效期）

Li Na：Well，could you give me more details?

Mr. Zhang：No problem. Generally our price is negotiable，but in negotiation，you need to take notice of the current exchange rate. The discount should also be within our capability.

（一般，我们的价格是可以商量的，但要注意在磋商中要关注汇率因素。折扣也要在我们可以承受的范围之内）

Li Na：I see，are there anything we need to pay more attention to?

Mr. Zhang：Yes. When it comes to terms of payment，a lot of things have to be considered. We have practiced different payment methods treating different types of customers，and we are going to know more about it later.

（我们对于不同类型的客户采用不同的付款方式，这些我们将在以后专门学习）

Li Na：And the date?

Mr. Zhang：It seems complicated and easy to confuse. In general，you just see to it that the dates have to conform to the contract of the terms.

（这看上去比较复杂且容易混淆。你只要记得日期必须与合同中的条款一致就行了）

Li Na：All right. I'll put them down.

Mr. Zhang：Oh，finally you'd better give an expression of thanks for the enquiry，hoping that the offer will be accepted.

（最后记得表达对对方询盘的谢意，希望报盘可以被对方接受）

Li Na：Thank you，Mr. Zhang.

After the conversation with Mr. Zhang，Li Na writes the following offer by herself.

Dear Mr. Johnson，

Thank you very much for your enquiry of April 1 for our 100% Cashmere Sweaters. We are now making you a firm offer subject to your reply reaching us before April 30，2012.

Men's	large	US $50.00 per piece
	medium	US $48.00 per piece
	small	US $45.00 per piece
Women's	large	US $47.00 per piece
	medium	US $45.00 per piece
	small	US $43.00 per piece

The above prices are based on CIF Vancouver，and the offer is valid for 7 days and is subject to our final confirmation.

Payment：by confirmed irrevocable L/C payable by draft at sight.
Shipment：June/July，2012 provided the L/C reaches us one month before the time of shipment.

We are glad to inform you that our products are selling fast because of their unique design and superior quality. Our factories are fully committed for months ahead; we suggest you place your order as soon as possible.

We are looking forward to hearing from you soon.

Yours faithfully,
Li Na

In two days, Li Na receives a counter-offer from the customer.

Dear Ms. Li,

Thank you for your letter of April 7, in which you offered us 100% Cashmere Sweaters.

Regrettably, we are unable to accept your offers as your prices are too high. We also have similar offers from Korean maker. They are 25% lower than yours.

We like the quality and design of your products. We admit that the quality of your products is better, but it does not justify such a large difference in price.

We might not do business with you unless you could make us some discount, say 20%, on your prices.

We hope you will consider our counter-offer most favorably and let us have your reply soon.

Yours faithfully,
Mike Johnson

After receiving the letter, Li Na doesn't know what to do next. Then she goes to Mr. Zhang for help again.

Li Na: Mr. Zhang, I've received a counter-offer from customer. They think the given price is too high to accept and they expect that we can offer a 20% discount on that price.

Mr. Zhang: I've known about it. As the quantity demanded is relatively low, we can provide 15% discount only.

Li Na: Then, should I reject directly?

Mr. Zhang: It is not a one-shot business in negotiation，but requires several rounds of talk to get a satisfactory bargain for both parties. We have various kinds of products and we can recommend some other products to the customers.

Li Na: I see. Thank you.

李娜再次拟了一份发盘给客户：给客户看上的产品打八五折，顺带推荐其他产品。

Here is an offer from Li Na.

Dear Johnson，

Your counter-offer of 20% discount for 100% Cashmere Sweater is beyond our margin. Our special offer for this classic style is 15% discount at most.

As you know，we are the largest cashmere manufacturer in China and our products are up to the standard and trend.

As another choice，we would like to recommend you some other products. We provide the following cashmere series items：

    100% Cashmere Knit Sweaters

    Ladies' 100% Cashmere Knitwear

    Men's 100% Cashmere Knitwear

    100% Cashmere Scarves 150 cm×30 cm Tartans

    100% Cashmere Shawls 190 cm×70 cm

These can be customized into 85% silk 15% cashmere or blended cashmere. If you have interest in these products，we can give you special offer.

Looking forward to your reply.

Yours sincerely，

Li Na

很快，客户再次还盘，表示对八五折的价格还是不满意，但是非常满意李娜推荐的另外一款产品，希望她能将该产品的具体信息多发一些过来，公司会在近期订货。

Here is the Counter-offer from customer.

Dear Li Na，

As for your last firm offer of 15% discount for cashmere，we cannot accept.

But in the attached recommendation list，we have some interest to know 100% Cashmere Scarves 150 cm×30 cm Tartans and 100% Cashmere Shawls 190 cm×70 cm and about its customization service. I hope you can send us more information about the two items and expect you can give us the most special offer.

Our demand is immediate and will place a large order.

Looking forward to your reply.

Yours sincerely，
Mike Johnson

李娜终于看到了这些天发盘和还盘的成果，开心地准备回复客户的要求。
张先生按照惯例为李娜准备了一些巩固练习。

 Practice 小·练习

Task 1：Answer the following questions.

1. What are offers and counter-offers?

   _____

2. What four elements must be covered in an offer?

   _____

3. Are there any other details need to be mentioned in an offer letter?

   _____

Task 2：Supply the missing words in the blanks to make the letter complete.

June 6，2012

Dear Sirs，

We are pleased to _____1_____ your enquiry dated May 25，2012 and as requested，we are sending you under separate cover, a copy of our catalog, latest _____2_____ list，together with our sample books. Details of our condition of sale and terms of _____3_____ are stated therein.

Our Cotton Tablecloths are enjoying fast sales in the United States and Europe because they are ____4____ excellent in quality ____5____ reasonable in price.

We are looking ____6____ to your order.

Yours faithfully,
Mary Clark

Task 3: Fill in the blanks with proper terms.
1. After receiving their enquiry, we sent them a _____.
2. We take pleasure _____ writing to you.
3. This offer is firm _____ _____ your early reply.
4. Please quote us your lowest price CIF New York _____ shipment _____ May.
5. We assure you _____ immediate shipment.
6. We are _____ for your early reply.

Task 4: Choose the best answer.
(　) 1. Please _____ us your lowest prices for both men's and women's winter jackets.
    A. offer   B. quote   C. supply
(　) 2. Please _____ us 500 glass vases CIF Qingdao, China.
    A. offer   B. quote   C. supply
(　) 3. This is our best price, _____ which we have already concluded several transactions with your competitors.
    A. in   B. of   C. at
(　) 4. Enclosed please find our quotation sheet _____ different sizes and colors of our banners.
    A. covering   B. covered   C. covers
(　) 5. Sellers prefer to wait till the price goes _____.
    A. down   B. stably   C. up
(　) 6. The offer is to be _____ if it is not accepted by the end of this month.
    A. withdraw   B. withdrew   C. withdrawn
(　) 7. Please quote us your lowest price and tell us when you could make shipment if an order should _____ with your firm.
    A. be placed   B. be put   C. be sent

（　　）8. Please let us know _____ the lowest prices at which you can execute this order，CIF Boston.

A．in return　　　B．by return　　　C．on return

 Comments & Suggestions 评价及建议

李娜出色地完成了四项任务，现在要求她熟练掌握以下单词与词组。

1. available [əˈveɪləbl] *a*. 可得的；空闲的
2. transaction [trænˈzækʃən] *n*. 交易；事务
3. relevant [ˈrelɪvənt] *a*. 有关的；中肯的
4. disagreement [ˌdɪsəˈɡriːmənt] *n*. 不一致；争论；意见不同
5. amendment [əˈmendmənt] *n*. 改善；改正
6. limitation [ˌlɪmɪˈteɪʃən] *n*. 限制；限度；有效期限
7. properly [ˈprɒpəlɪ] *adv*. 适当地；正确地；恰当地
8. essential [ɪˈsenʃəl] *a*. 基本的；必要的
9. element [ˈelɪmənt] *n*. 元素；要素
10. discount [ˈdɪskaunt] *n*. 折扣
11. payment [ˈpeɪmənt] *n*. 支付
12. indication [ˌɪndɪˈkeɪʃən] *n*. 指示，指出
13. packing [ˈpækɪŋ] *n*. 包装；填充物
14. carriage [ˈkærɪdʒ] *n*. 运输；运费
15. insurance [ɪnˈʃuərəns] *n*. 保险；保险费
16. quotation [kwəʊˈteɪʃən] *n*. （贸易）报价单
17. considerate [kənˈsɪdərɪt] *a*. 体贴的；体谅的；考虑周到的
18. attitude [ˈætɪtjuːd] *n*. 态度

19. superior [suːˈpɪərɪə] *a*. 上级的；优秀的，出众的
20. item [ˈaɪtəm] *n*. 条款；项目；一件商品（或物品）
21. willingness [ˈwɪlɪŋnɪs] *n*. 自愿，乐意
22. period [ˈpɪərɪəd] *n*. 时期；（一段）时间
23. validity [vəˈlɪdɪtɪ] *n*. 有效，合法性
24. negotiable [nɪˈɡəʊʃəbl] *a*. 可谈判的；可协商的；（票据）可兑现的
25. alternative [ɔːlˈtɜːnətɪv] *a*. 两者择一的
26. capability [ˌkeɪpəˈbɪlɪtɪ] *n*. 才能，能力；生产率
27. competitor [kəmˈpetɪtə] *n*. 竞争者；对手
28. complicated [ˈkɒmplɪkeɪtɪd] *a*. 结构复杂的；混乱的，麻烦的
29. conform [kənˈfɔːm] *v*. 符合；遵照；适应环境
30. Vancouver [vænˈkuːvə] *n*. [地名]（加拿大）温哥华
31. shipment [ˈʃɪpmənt] *n*. 装运；载货量
32. margin [ˈmɑːdʒɪn] *n*. 利润，盈余
33. justify [ˈdʒʌstɪfaɪ] *v*. 证明……有理；对……作出解释
34. one-shot [ˈwʌnʃɒt] *a*. 只有一次的

35. manufacturer [ˌmænjʊˈfæktʃərə]
    n. 制造商,制造厂;厂主
36. standard [ˈstændəd] n. 标准,规格
    a. 标准的,合格的
37. trend [trend] n. 走向;趋向
38. dominate [ˈdɒmɪneɪt] v. 控制;

在……中占首要地位
39. customize [ˈkʌstəmaɪz] vt. 定制,
    定做;按规格改制
40. blend [blend] v. 混合;把……掺
    在一起

1. figure out　发现,明白
2. exchange rate　汇率
3. firm offer　实盘
4. final confirmation　最终确认

Knowledge Consolidation 知识点巩固

　　李娜利用休息时间查找了一些与发盘和还盘相关的句型,以及发盘与还盘的注意要点,以备将来可用,整理如下:

I. Useful sentence patterns.

1. We will make you a firm offer as soon as possible. 我们将尽快向你方报实盘。

2. Our offer is firm for three days. 我方报盘有效期为三天。

3. We're making you a firm offer as follows, subject to your reply reaching us by the end of this week. 现向你方报实盘如下,以你方答复于本周末前到达为有效。

4. The offer is subject to our final confirmation. 本报盘以我方最后确认为准。

5. The offer is subject to change without notice. 本报盘以可以随时更改而无需另作通知为条件。

6. Our products have obtained unanimous approval. 我们的产品得到了一致的认可。

7. Your counter-offer is not in line with the international market price. 你方还盘与国际市场价格不符。

8. We cannot entertain your suggestion because it does not seem workable. 我们不能考虑接受你方的建议,因为此建议似乎不可行。

9. We demand immediate delivery. 我们要求立即交货。

10. The buyer demands the seller to ship the goods within a month. 买方要求卖方在一个月内发货。

11. Your proposal has met with general approval. 你的建议得到了一致同意。

12. Please pay by . . ./Please make the payment by . . . 请用……方式付款。

13. For 100% of the invoice value. 按发票金额的 100%。

14. Please quote the lowest price CFR Singapore for 500 Flying Pigeon brand bicycles. 请报 500 辆飞鸽牌自行车成本加运费至新加坡最低价。

15. In view of our long-standing business relationship, we would like to allow you another 2% commission for further promotion of our products. 考虑到我们之间长期的贸

国际商务英语函电

易关系,我们愿再给你方百分之二的佣金,以进一步推销我们的产品。

16. We shall remit you a 5% commission of invoice value after payment effected. 货款支付后,我们将按发票金额的百分之五汇给你方佣金。

17. Please grant us a 4% commission as a special consideration. 请特殊照顾给我们百分之四的佣金。

18. We will give you back a 5% commission by check. 我们将用支票方式支付你方百分之五的佣金。

II. Three points should be considered when you make an offer.

1	It must be written clearly whether the offer is firm or not.
2	The offer must indicate all the main terms and conditions of the transaction.
3	The offer must state the time of validity.

III. A counter-offer letter must be handled with great care and both parties must keep in mind that they value their friendship and future business. The letter should be written this way:

1	Express appreciation for the customer's effort in making an offer.
2	Express regret that you cannot accept the offer and explain the reasons.
3	Make a suggestion about your own terms and conditions to the counter-offer.
4	Express your desire to the reader, hoping that your counter-offer will be accepted.

Task: Translate the following sentences into Chinese.

1. Our offer is a firm offer and remains good until 2:30 p.m. August 20, 2012, Beijing time.

   _____

2. We trust that you will be able to accept our offer, which shall be kept open against reply by cable.

   _____

3. We regret to inform you that the goods required by you are not available for the time being, and for this reason we are unable to send you an offer at this moment.

   _____

4. The size of our order depends greatly on your price.

   _____

5. Here is our official offer for each item, CIF Amsterdam.

   _____

国际商务英语函电

Congratulations!

You have completed all the tasks above by yourself.

Please go on to the next unit.

Unit 6　Orders and Contracts

Part 1　Orders

Situational Introduction 情景介绍

李娜今天收到了一封 email,随信还附带了一张货物订单。她很开心,却不知道该如何处理这份订单,于是向带教老师张先生进行咨询。张先生帮助李娜一起查看了这封 email(如下),并向李娜解释了订单的含义及订单书写的相关技巧。

Dear Sirs,

We thank you for your letter of July 2 and are glad to inform you that your samples are satisfactory. Enclosed please find our Order No. 237 for four of the items.

All these items are urgently required by our customers. We, therefore, hope you will arrange delivery at an early date. We expect to find a good market for your goods and hope to place further and large orders with you in the near future.

Yours faithfully,
Michael

Order No. 237

Quantity	Item	Catalog No.	Price
250	Bed Sheets, 106 cm, blue	75	$5 each
250	Bed Sheets, 120 cm, primrose	82	$3 each
500	Pillow Cases, blue	117	$2 a pair
500	Pillow Cases, primrose	121	$2 a pair

Packing: In cotton cloth bales.
Shipment: Prompt shipment from Shanghai.
Payment: By irrevocable L/C available by draft at sight.

国际商务英语函电

Knowledge to Impart 知识传授

Mr. Zhang: Li Na，this letter is a kind of **order letter** which means **an oral or written buying promise**. An order should at least contain the following points:

- description of the commodity，such as specification，size，quantity，quality，and article number（if any）;
- prices（unit prices as well as total prices）;
- terms of payment;
- mode of packing;
- port of shipment，port of destination and time of shipment，etc.

（订单是一种买方口头或者书面的购买承诺。订单必须包含以下几点：货物的详细说明，比如规格、大小、数量、质量以及货号；货物的价格（单价和总价）；付款方式；包装方式；目的港及装运期等）

The following structure can be for your reference in placing an order:

1. Use direct language in the first paragraph to tell the seller of the buyer's intention to place an order.
2. Describe what is being ordered in great detail. Indicate the catalog numbers，sizes，colors，prices，specifications and all other relevant information that will enable the seller to fill the order without any questions.
3. Close the letter by expressing willingness to cooperate or suggesting future business dealings.

（书写订单时的参考结构如下：

1. 在第一段使用直接、简单的语言将买方下订单的意愿告诉卖方。
2. 详细说明需要订购的产品信息，说明产品的货号、大小、颜色、价格等其他相关信息，这些信息可以使卖方正确供货。
3. 在信的结尾处，表达出合作的意愿或暗示今后想要继续业务往来）

 Practice 小练习

Let's help Li Na finish the three tasks together.

Task 1: Answer the following questions.

1. What do we call the email Li Na has received today?

   _____

2. What are the important points when writing an order letter?

   _____

Task 2: According to the order letter, fill in the blanks.

1. The order number is _____ .
2. The goods to be ordered are _____ .

3. The total number of the goods are _____ .
4. The total prices of the goods are _____ .
5. The mode of packing is _____ .
6. The time of shipment is _____ .
7. The terms of payment is _____ .

Task 3: Complete the following table with the information in the order letter.

Writing Steps　写作步骤	Expressions　表达方式
1. 感谢对方的来函，决定订购货物	
2. 订购商品的名称、规格、数量、单价、总值等	
3. 说明你所希望的交易方式（包装、装运期及付款方式等）	
4. 表示若对本次交易满意，以后会继续订购	

Comments & Suggestions 评价及建议

李娜出色地完成了三项任务，现在要求她熟练掌握以下单词与词组。

1. inform [ɪnˈfɔːm] v. 通知，告知
2. sample [ˈsæmpl] n. 样例，样张
3. satisfactory [ˌsætɪsˈfæktərɪ] a. 令人感到满意的
4. urgent [ˈɜːdʒənt] a. 急切的，迫切的
5. specification [ˌspesɪfɪˈkeɪʃən] n. 规格，产品说明
6. quantity [ˈkwɒntɪtɪ] n. 数量
7. destination [ˌdestɪˈneɪʃən] n. 目的地
8. enclosed [ɪnˈkləʊzd] a. 随信附上
9. pillow [ˈpɪləʊ] n. 枕头
10. primrose [ˈprɪmrəʊz] a. 淡黄色的
11. bale [beɪl] n. 大包
12. L/C (letter of credit) n. 信用证
13. commodity [kəˈmɒdɪtɪ] n. 商品，货物

· ·

1. order No.　订单号
2. make delivery　发货
3. at an early date　早期
4. place an order　下订单
5. bed sheet　床单
6. pillow case　枕头套
7. cotton cloth bale　棉布大包
8. irrevocable L/C　不可撤销信用证
9. draft at sight　即期汇票
10. terms of payment　付款方式

Mr. Zhang： I will show you another order letter to give you more ideas about it.

Dear sirs,

From the samples you sent us in April, we have made selections and have the pleasure of giving you the following order on usual terms for shipment to Sydney.

Quantity	Item	Catalog Number	Price
150 cartons	Health Tea	T16	US $110 per carton
250 cartons	Wen Jing Tea	T17	US $120 per carton
350 cartons	Fat Reducing Tea	T18	US $130 per carton

For your information, we have applied for the import license and the letter of credit for this order. Since we need the goods urgently, you are requested to effect shipment one month after receipt of our L/C. There is a good market for the said items, and if this initial order is satisfactorily executed, we are prepared to place repeat orders with you in the near future.

We are awaiting your confirmation and prompt delivery.

Yours faithfully,
James

Li Na： Thank you, Mr. Zhang, I have learned a lot about the order today.

 Knowledge Consolidation 知识点巩固

我们和李娜一样,将来多是国际贸易行业的从业人员,在张先生的指导下,我们学到了什么? 是否掌握了下订单的基本步骤呢? 我们是否能准确地书写一封订单信件呢? 让我们一起来试试吧!

Useful sentence patterns：

1. We find both the price and quality of your products satisfactory and are pleased to give you an order for the following items on the understanding that they will be supplied from current stock at the prices named. (我们对你方产品的价格和质量都很满意,现寄上订单一份,订购下列产品,要求按指定价格以现货供应)

2. We thank you for your quotation of February 20 and enclose herewith our order No. 56 for the goods. As the goods are urgently required by our customers, we hope you will deliver them promptly. (感谢你方2月20日的报价,随函附上56号订单。因我方客户急需该货,希望能尽快装运)

3. We are pleased to give you an order for ... (我们非常高兴向您订购……)

4. We herewith order the following items ... （在此订购下列产品……）

5. Enclosed please find our order. /Our order is enclosed.（随信附上订单）

6. We would be grateful if you could deliver as soon as possible.（请尽快交货，我们将非常感激）

7. Packing should be strong enough to ensure sufficient protection.（包装要足够结实，以确保为产品提供足够的保护）

8. Payment shall be rendered upon delivery.（货到付款）

Task 1：Read the following order letter and match the Chinese expressions with the English ones.

Dear Mr. Warner，

We have received your price list and the sample. We would like to place the following order with you：

Commodity：	DVD Player
Specification：	Panasonic DVD - LS50
Quantity：	3,000
Price：	$254.00 each
Date of shipment：	By 20th July，2012
Payment：	By L/C

Please confirm acceptance of our order by return mail and send an advice of shipment. We will forward the bank draft upon receipt of them.

Yours sincerely，

Karl Davis

Karl Davis

(   ) 1. 价格表   a. commodity

(   ) 2. 银行汇票   b. specification

(   ) 3. 回信确认订货   c. sample

(   ) 4. 数量   d. price list

(   ) 5. 规格   e. date of shipment

(   ) 6. 样品   f. quantity

(   ) 7. 商品（名）   g. place the following order with you

(   ) 8. 装运期   h. L/C (letter of credit)

(   ) 9. 向贵公司订购以下货物   i. confirm acceptance of the order by return mail

(   )10. 信用证   j. bank draft

Task 2：Write an order letter using the information given below.

假设你公司收到了 ABC 公司数码照相机的价格表和样品，对报价和样品质量感到满意,决定订购。请你写一封订购信,告诉对方订购数量、价格、装运期和付款方式,并希望对方回函确认订购。

Dear Mr. Zhang,

_____

_____

_____

_____

Yours faithfully,

(Signature)_____

Part 2　Contracts

Situational Introduction 情景介绍

　　一周后的一天,李娜收到了 Edward 先生传真过来的订单,这将是她独立处理的第一份订单:丹麦的 ABC 外贸公司决定订购 10,000 件 T 恤衫。以下是订单的部分内容。

ABC Trading Co. Ltd.
Kollegievej 6,9000 Alborg, Denmark
Tel：+ 45 43 31 32 33
Fax：+ 45 43 31 32 43

Date：August 15,2012

Shanghai Industry & Trade Co. Ltd.
Room 1106, No. 777 Lu Jia Zui Road, Pudong New Area, Shanghai, China

Dear Miss Li,
　　We are glad to order from you your T-shirts ...

Yours faithfully,
Justin Edward

李娜现在要做的就是根据订单的内容,亲自填制一份销售合同,该怎么填呢?

 Knowledge to Impart 知识传授

Let's help Li Na with the following three questions.

Question 1:What is a contract?

Answer:A contract is an agreement **accepted by law**,by which two parties **mutually promise** to buy or sell some particular goods,or to do a certain work.(合同是一份**双方都同意**买卖某种商品或共同去做某件事情,并具有**法律效力**的协议)

Question 2:How many parts can a sales contract be divided into? What are they?

Answer:A sales contract can be divided into three parts —— **preamble,body and witness clauses**.(合同通常分为三部分:**约首、正文和约尾**)

Preamble includes:

1. name and number(合同的名称和编号);

2. each party's name,nationality,principal places of business,telephone or fax number(签约各方名称、国籍、法定地址、电话或传真);

3. date of signing(签约日期).

Body mainly includes:

1. name of goods(货物的品名);

2. quality and specifications(质量和规格);

3. quantity(数量);

4. price(价格);

5. terms of payment(支付条件);

6. packing(包装);

7. shipment & delivery(装运与发货);

8. insurance(保险).

注:事实上,正文部分还包括 inspection(检验)、claim(索赔)、arbitration(仲裁)、force majeure(不可抗力)等内容,这里不作具体填写要求。

Witness clauses include:

1. concluding Sentences(结束语);

2. signature(签字);

3. seal(盖章).

Question 3:Some companies use sales contracts and others use sales confirmations. Are there any differences?

Answer:A sales contract and a sales confirmation actually play the same role in trading.(销售合同和销售确认书所起到的作用是完全相同的)

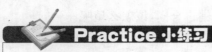

Task 1: Fill in the preamble of the sales contract according to the letter on Page 57.

Sales Contract

Contract No.：DS - 200018

Shanghai Date：August 15，2012

This contract is made by and between

Seller：Shanghai Industry & Trade Co. Ltd.

Add：_____1_____

Tel：0086 - 21 - 58876721

Fax：0086 - 21 - 58876723

and Buyer：_____2_____

Add：_____3_____

The seller agrees to sell and the buyer agrees to buy the undermentioned goods according to the terms and conditions below：

...

Task 2: The following is the body part of a sales contract. Please finish it with the correct names of terms and conditions.

Sales Contract

...

The seller agrees to sell and the buyer agrees to buy the undermentioned goods according to the terms and conditions below：

1. _____ : T-shirts
2. _____ : short-sleeved, 100% cotton, with color white, black, blue and red
3. _____ : 10,000 (2,500 pieces for each color)
4. _____ : keep it out of water/rain（防潮）
5. _____ : USD 10 for each, CIF Alborg Denmark
   _____ : USD 100,000
6. _____ : By irrevocable L/C payable at sight. The L/C should reach the seller 30 days before the time of shipment and to remain valid for negotiation in China until the 15th day after the day of shipment（凭不可撤销即期信用证付款,于装运期前30天开到卖方,并于上述装运期后15天内在中国议付有效）
7. Shipment mark：KTC 180
   _____ : during August，2012

国际商务英语函电

_____ ：Huangpu, China

Port of destination：Alborg，Denmark

8. _____ ：To be covered by the buyer

Task 3：Which of the following sentences can be put into the witness clauses? The correct answer may be more than one.

A. Enclosed please also find our latest illustrated catalog for other products.

B. We'd like to place a trial order with you.

C. The seller agrees to sell and the buyer agrees to buy the undermentioned goods according to the terms and conditions below.

D. If you find any other products interesting，please let us know.

E. We have reached an agreement on Packing and Quality.

F. If we again fail to receive your L/C in time，we shall have to cancel our sales confirmation.

G. We will send you our best quotation.

通过以上三项练习,李娜已经对销售合同的三部分了解得很清楚了,那么,随合同附上的函电又应该如何措辞呢? 我们与李娜一起完成下一个练习吧,做完你就会明白了。

Task 4：Fill in each blank with a proper word.

Dear Sirs，

We have booked your order No. 237 ____1____ our Container Bags and we are sending you herewith our Sales Contract No. 222 ____2____ duplicate. Please sign and return one copy ____3____ our file.

It is understood that a letter of credit in our favor ____4____ the above-mentioned goods will be established immediately. Please see ____5____ it that the stipulations in the L/C should strictly conform with ____6____ stated in the contract so as to avoid subsequent amendments. You may rest assured that shipment will be effected ____7____ the least possible delay as soon as we have received the L/C.

Thank you very much for your cooperation and look forward to further orders ____8____ you.

Yours faithfully，

×××

国际商务英语函电

Comments & Suggestions 评价及建议

李娜出色地完成了四项任务,现在要求她熟练掌握以下单词与词组。

1. mutually ['mjuːtʃʊəlɪ] *adv.* 相互地
2. agreement [ə'griːmənt] *n.* 协议
3. preamble [priː'æmbl] *n.* 约首
4. shipment ['ʃɪpmənt] *n.* 装运
5. confirmation [ˌkɒnfə'meɪʃən] *n.* 确认
6. valid ['vælɪd] *a.* 有效的
7. herewith [hɪə'wɪð] *adv.* 同此
8. covering ['kʌvərɪŋ] *a.* 涉及……的
9. stipulation [ˌstɪpjʊ'leɪʃən] *n.* 规定
10. subsequent ['sʌbsɪkwənt] *a.* 后来的
11. inspection [ɪn'spekʃən] *n.* 检验
12. claim [kleɪm] *n.* 索赔
13. arbitration [ˌɑːbɪ'treɪʃn] *n.* 仲裁
14. seal [siːl] *n.* 盖章
15. undermentioned ['ʌndə'menʃənd] *a.* 下述的
16. illustrate ['ɪləstreɪt] *v.* 说明;表明;给……加插图
17. trial ['traɪəl] *n.* 试验 *a.* 试验的

1. order *sth.* from *sb.* 向某人订购某物
2. witness clauses 约尾
3. port of destination 到达港
4. force majeure 不可抗力
5. in duplicate 一式两份
6. for our file 以便我们存档
7. in one's favor/in favor of 对……有益
8. see to it that 一定做到
9. conform with 与……保持一致
10. may rest assured 请放心

 ## Knowledge Consolidation 知识点巩固

让我们通过以下练习巩固本单元的重点吧!

请大家先阅读以下中文销售合同,再将英文销售合同填写完整(合同里没有提到的内容,不作填写要求)。

销售合同

合同号:AC 4789
卖方:北京轻工业进出口公司
买方:纽约贸易公司
商品名称:永久牌自行车
规格:MB28 型

数量：1,000 辆
单价：CIF 纽约每辆 70 美元
总值：70,000 美元
包装：木箱装
装运期：2012 年 9 月 30 日前自中国港口至纽约，允许分批装运和装船
付款条件：凭不可撤销即期信用证付款，于装运期前一个月开到卖方，并于上述装运期后 15 天内在中国议付有效
保险：由买方支付

Sales Contract

Contract No.：_____1_____

_____2_____：Beijing Light Industrial Import & Export Corporation

Buyer：_____3_____

The seller agrees to sell and the buyer agrees to buy the undermentioned goods according to the terms and conditions below：

_____4_____："Forever" brand bicycles

Quality and _____5_____：_____6_____

_____7_____：1,000 bicycles

Unit price：_____8_____

Total value：_____9_____

_____10_____：In wooden cases

_____11_____：To be effected not later than _____12_____, allowing partial shipment and transhipment

Port of shipment：_____13_____

Port of destination：_____14_____

_____15_____：By irrevocable L/C payable at sight. The L/C should reach the seller one month before the time of shipment and to remain valid for negotiation in China until the 15th day after the day of shipment

_____16_____：To be covered by the buyer

Congratulations！
You have completed all the tasks above by yourself.
Please go on to the next unit.

国际商务英语函电

Unit 7   Payment

Situational Introduction 情景介绍

在短暂的实习后,李娜发现在国际贸易中完成交易的标志是由完成付款这一环节来体现的,于是她翻看了一些资料,了解关于付款方式的有关知识。在任何交易中,双方一旦达成意向后就要讨论如何支付的问题,毕竟支付的成功实现才是买卖成功的最终标志。然而,和国内贸易相比,国际贸易支付要复杂和困难得多。

李娜还是有很多的困惑,如:国际贸易中有哪些支付方式? 各有哪些优劣? 如何在外贸函电中准确表达? 在学习之前先来一起讨论一个小问题吧!

Group Discussion 1

What do you think are the reasons for the complexities and difficulties in international payment?

Knowledge to Impart 知识传授

Mr. Zhang: In international trade, there are mainly five types of payment: **Open Account, Payment-in-advance, Remittance, Collection** and **Letter of Credit**. Different methods of payment are adopted, depending mainly on the relationship between the seller and the buyer.

(国际贸易货款的支付方式多种多样:赊账、预先付款、汇付、托收和信用证是常用的五种方式)

1. Open Account

Open Account means goods are shipped and documents remitted directly to the buyer with a request for payment from the buyer at an appropriate time.

(赊账方式是指卖方先发货和传送有关单据给买方,并在未来的某一时间收回货款的付款方式)

This payment method is advantageous to the buyer but most risky for the seller, thus it is only used between long-term relationship business partners.

(这种付款方式对买方最有利而对卖方风险最大,因此它仅在双方具有长期合作关系的情况下使用)

2. Payment-in-advance

Payment-in-advance terms or prepayment terms call for payment to the seller **before** the buyer has received the product.

（预先付款要求买方在收到货物之前付款给卖方）

These terms are the **least** risky payment method for the seller and the **most** risky for the buyer. Not surprisingly，prepayment terms are not typically used in normal trade.

（这样的付款方式对卖方是最安全的,但对买方来说是最有风险的。所以预先付款方式在正常的贸易中不常用也不足为奇了）

3. Remittance

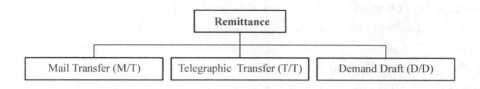

Remittance，as the simplest method of payment in international trade，means that a bank，at the request of its customer，transfer a certain sum of money to its overseas branch or correspondent bank，instructing it to pay a named person in that country.

（汇付是付款人通过银行,把款项汇给收款人的支付方式）

There are generally three types of Remittance：**Mail Transfer**（M/T），**Telegraphic Transfer**（T/T），and **Demand Draft**（D/D）.

（汇付主要包括信汇、电汇和票汇三种方式）

Mail transfer and telegraphic transfer both refer to the movement of money from one bank account to another. Mail transfer is cheap but slow，so it is typically used for remittance of small sums or of little urgency.

（信汇和电汇都是指将钱款从一个银行账户转到另一个账户。信汇费用低廉,但邮寄信件速度太慢,资金在途时间长,收款迟缓,因此这种方式现在仅用于小额汇款或对汇付时间要求不高的情况）

Telegraphic transfer is safe and fast，thus it is currently the most popular way of remitting funds.

（电汇速度最快,且安全可靠）

Demand draft is a draft drawn by the importer's bank on its branch or correspondent bank in the exporter's country and is payable immediately when the exporter demands payment.

（票汇是由进口商的银行示意它在出口商国家的分行或联系行开出的见票即付的付款方式）

4. Collection

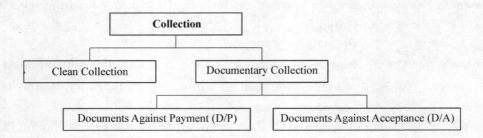

A collection refers to an arrangement whereby the seller draws a draft on the buyer and authorizes its bank to collect the money from the buyer.

（托收是指由卖方开具汇票，委托所在地银行通过买方当地银行向买方收款）

Under a collection，the seller ships the goods，prepares the draft and/or shipping documents，and submits the draft and/or shipping documents to its bank for collection of the proceeds. The commonly-used collection is documentary collection.

A documentary collection refers to the process by which the exporter submits drafts accompanied by shipping documents to his bank for collecting proceeds from the importer.

There are two types of documentary collection：Documents against Payment（D/P） and Documents against Acceptance（D/A）.

（托收分光票托收和跟单托收两种：最常用的跟单托收根据交单条件的不同，分为付款交单和承兑交单）

D/P calls for actual payment against transfer of shipping documents. There are D/P at sight and D/P after sight.

（付款交单又分为即期和远期两种）

The former requires immediate payment by the importer to get hold of the documents. In the latter condition，the importer is given a certain period to make payment at 30，45，60 or 90 days after presentation of the documents.

（前者要求进口方立即付款以取得有关单据，后者则给予进口方一段时间付款，通常是 30 天、45 天、60 天或者 90 天）

5. Letter of Credit（L/C）

The letter of credit used in international trade should always be accompanied by export documents or shipping documents，so it is called the documentary letter of credit，or simply the documentary credit.

（信用证的使用通常伴随着出口单据或运输单据的使用，所以也被称为跟单信用证）

The most widely-used method of payment in international trade is the letter of credit （L/C），which is reliable and safe for both sellers and buyers. We will discuss this payment method next time.

（信用证是国际贸易中最普遍使用的支付方式，对买卖双方来说，既可靠又安全）

Notes：

1. payment [ˈpeɪmənt] *n*. 支付；支付的款

   payer [ˈpeɪə] *n*. 付款人，支付者　payee [peɪˈiː] *n*. 收款人

   terms of payment/payment terms/modes of payment　付款方式，付款条件

   make payment/effect payment　支付，付款

   payment in advance　预付货款

   payment on delivery　货到付款

   deferred payment（payment on deferred terms）　延期付款

   cash payment　现金付款

   payment by L/C　凭信用证付款

   in payment of　付某种费用的款（如：发票、费用、佣金等）

   in payment for　付某种具体实物的款（如：广告、商品、样品等）

   e. g. （1）We enclose a cheque for USD 2,000 in payment of all commissions due
   to you.

   　　　（2）We have received your check for EUR 3,000 in payment for the Carpets
   ordered by you.

2. remit [rɪˈmɪt] *v*. 汇款

   remittance [rɪˈmɪtəns] *n*. 汇款（后接介词 for 和金额，前面常用动词 make, send；
   remittance 前面可以加冠词 a/the）

   e. g. （1）We are sending you our remittance for $500 to cover the incidental expenses.

   　　　（2）On receipt of your remittance，please acknowledge.

   mail transfer（M/T）　信汇

   e. g. As the value of this order is rather small，we hope you could agree to your making
   payment by M/T after receipt of the documents.（由于交易额甚小，希望贵方同意
   我方在收到单证后以信汇方式付款）

   telegraphic transfer（T/T）　电汇

   bill of exchange　汇票

   reverse remittance　逆汇

   draft　汇票（汇票的正式名称是 bill of exchange,简称 bill,但一般用 draft）

   clean draft　光票

   sight draft　即期汇票

   time draft　远期汇票

   D/D = demand draft = bank draft = banker's cheque　银行开的即期汇票，效力等同于
   现金

   draft at 30(60,90,120) days' sight　30(60,90,120)天远期汇票

   documentary draft　跟单汇票

   accept/honor a draft　承兑汇票

   dishonor a draft　拒付汇票

3. collection [kəˈlekʃən] 托收

　clean collection　光票托收

　documentary collection　跟单托收

　D/P（documents against payment）　付款交单

　D/A（documents against acceptance）　承兑交单

　D/P at sight　即期付款交单

　D/P after sight　远期付款交单

听完张先生的讲解，你们懂了多少？下面大家来讨论一下这些问题吧！

 Group Discussion 2

1. How many modes of payment are there in international trade?
2. What is the main difference between D/P and D/A?
3. What is the disadvantage of payment by remittance and collection?
4. What is the advantage of payment by L/C?
5. What is the generally-used mode of payment in international trade? Why?

　　具备以上三种常用国际贸易支付方式的基本知识后，张先生继续用实例来讲解如何将这些知识应用到具体的外贸函电中。常用的搭配和句型需要会熟练使用哦！

Mr. Zhang：Li Na，please read the following specimen letters to learn the useful writing structures.

Li Na：OK.

Letter 1：Asking for Direct Payment by the Buyer

Dear Mr. Smith，

　　We refer to your Contract No. 625 covering lumber in the amount of $800 and Contract No. 626 for iron pipe in the amount of $700.

　　Since both these contracts are less than $1,000 in value，we would like you to ship the goods to us on cash against documents（C. A. D）basis.

　　We trust that this arrangement will meet with your approval and await your early reply.

Yours sincerely，

×××

国际商务英语函电

Letter 2: Payment by T/T

Dear Sirs,

We have received your statement for the quarter ended on 30 September and found that it agrees with our books. As requested, we have instructed our bankers to send the sum of USD 5,000 by T/T for the credit of your account at the Bank of China, Shanghai Branch.

This payment clears your account up to August 31. The unpaid balance of USD 2,000 for the goods supplied during September will be faxed to our bankers on or before November 15.

Yours faithfully,

× × ×

Letter 3: Advising Establishment of L/C

Dear Sirs,

With regard to Sales Contract No. 301, we have instructed the Commonwealth Bank of Australia, Melbourne to open an irrevocable Letter of Credit No. 58 for USD 29,000 in your favor, valid until July 19.

A minimum of 600 dozen is required to be shipped not later than June 15, and the order must be shipped completely by June 31. If you can deliver the goods sooner, there is a good chance that we can send you substantial additional orders.

We are glad that we have been able to place this initial order for JS408 with you and trust the quality of the goods will prove to be first class in every respect. Enclosed please find the copy L/C No. 58.

We hope to hear favorably from you soon.

Yours faithfully,

× × ×

国际商务英语函电

Letter 4: Asking for D/A Payment

Dear Sirs,

Thank you for your letter of June 9 in which we have concluded a transaction of 3,000 dozen Nike brand shoes. But to our regret, you still ask for payment by confirmed irrevocable L/C as a rule.

Payment by L/C is rather inconvenient to a customer like us who place medium-sized orders. It will add to our cost and undoubtedly tie up our liquid funds for three or four months. This may cause delay in execution of the contract. The question becomes gnawing under present circumstances.

In view of our long business relationship and the small amount involved in this transaction, we hope you will extend us an easier payment terms as an exception, i.e. payment by D/A.

We shall highly appreciate your kindness in consideration of the above request and giving us a favorable reply.

Yours faithfully,

×××

Letter 5: Accepting Payment by D/P

Dear Sirs,

Thank you for your letter of 10 November, 2012 ordering 700 dozen glassware.

As far as the terms of payment are concerned, it is our usual practice to make payment on L/C basis. In view of the fact that it is the first transaction between us, we are prepared to accept payment by D/P at sight as an exception, but it should not be taken as a precedent. For future transactions, payment by L/C will be required. We have confidence that this trial order will turn out to the satisfaction of your customers.

We are looking forward to your confirmation.

Yours faithfully,

×××

Letter 6: Payment at 60 Days Sight

Dear Sirs,

We are pleased to inform you that arrangements have now been made to ship the washing machines you ordered on 22 May. The consignment will leave Shanghai by s.s. "Jenny", which is due to arrive at Port Klang sometime in late April.

In keeping with our usual terms of payment, we have drawn on you at 60 days and passed the draft and shipping documents to our banker. The documents will be presented to you by the Standard Chartered Bank against your acceptance of the draft in the usual way.

Yours faithfully,

× × ×

Letter 7: Insisting on Payment by L/C

Dear Sir/Madam,

Thank you for your fax of 19 March, 2012.

Although we have confidence in your integrity and ability, we wish to reiterate that our usual terms of payment by sight L/C remain unchanged in all our trade with new clients. Therefore, we regret being unable to accept your D/P terms. Maybe after several smooth and satisfactory transactions, we can consider other easier terms.

We are sorry to hear about the difficulties you are having, and understand the situation, but would appreciate it if you could accept the payment terms as soon as possible.

Our earthenware is well-known in the Southeast Asia market and most competitive in price, which, in our opinion, will help you a lot to stand firm in your market.

We look forward to your first order at an early date.

Yours truly,

× × ×

国际商务英语函电

Comments & Suggestions 评价及建议

李娜学习了以上信函,现在要求她掌握以下单词与词组。

1. covering ['kʌvərɪŋ] v. 关于
2. await [ə'weɪt] v. 等待
3. proposal [prə'pəʊzəl] n. 提议,建议
4. instruct [ɪn'strʌkt] v. 通知,指示
5. banker ['bæŋkə] n. 银行
6. substantial [səb'stænʃəl] a. 数量大的
7. initial [ɪ'nɪʃəl] a. 首次的
8. conclude [kən'kluːd] v. 达成,完成(交易)
9. execute ['eksɪkjuːt] v. 执行
10. gnawing ['nɔːɪŋ] a. 折磨人的,令人痛苦的
11. exception [ɪk'sepʃən] n. 例外
12. exceptional [ɪk'sepʃənl] a. 例外的
13. conducive [kən'djuːsɪv] a. 有助于……;有益于……
14. facilitate [fə'sɪlɪteɪt] v. 促进;帮助;使……容易
15. precedent ['presɪdənt] n. 先例
16. consignment [kən'saɪnmənt] n. 托运的货物
17. s. s. = steam ship [stiːmʃɪp] n. 轮船
18. draw [drɔː] v. 开出汇票
19. drawer ['drɔːə] n. 出票人,开汇票人
20. drawee [drɔː'iː] n. 受票人,付款人
21. reiterate [riː'ɪtəreɪt] v. 重申
22. earthenware ['ɜːθənˌweə] n. 陶器

1. in value 在价值上
2. on ... basis = on the basis of 以……为基础;按……条件
3. Cash Against Documents (C. A. D) 付款交单
4. Cash with Order (C. W. O) 随订单付现
5. Cash on Delivery (C. O. D) 交货付现/付现交单
6. meet with 满足
7. the unpaid balance 未付的余款
8. tie up 冻结
9. liquid funds 流动资金
10. on or before 截止
11. with regard to 关于
12. prove to be 证明是……
13. in view of 鉴于
14. easier payment terms 宽松的付款方式
15. under present circumstance 在目前情况下
16. as far as ... be concerned 关于……
17. usual practice 通常惯例
18. make payment 付款
19. trial order 试订单
20. shipping documents 装船单据
21. Standard Chartered Bank 渣打银行
22. regret doing sth. 对做过的事感到遗憾

国际商务英语函电

Practice 小·练习

Task 1: Match the following words with their Chinese meanings.

1. Import & Export License   a. 预先付款
2. collection   b. 信汇
3. time draft   c. 即期付款交单
4. payment in advance   d. 延期付款
5. M/T   e. 即期汇票
6. sight draft   f. 进出口许可证
7. drawee   g. 受票人
8. pay by cash   h. 托收
9. delay in payment   i. 远期汇票
10. D/P at sight   j. 现金付款

Task 2: Choose the best answer to complete each of the following sentences.

(   ) 1. Payment should _____ in time.

A. effect   B. be had   C. be effected   D. be effecting

(   ) 2. With regard to terms of payment, we regret to say that we only accept payment _____ documents.
A. by   B. for   C. against   D. on

(   ) 3. We shall draw on you by our documentary draft at sight, _____, without L/C.

A. in collection basis   B. on collection basis
C. by collection   D. on collecting basis

(   ) 4. _____ into consideration our business relations, we accept _____.
A. Take . . . payment by D/P   B. Taken . . . payment on D/P
C. Taking . . . payment by D/P   D. Takes . . . payment on D/P

(   ) 5. It was after repeated negotiations that we _____ the transaction at last.
A. did   B. concluded   C. come to   D. finish

(   ) 6. It is usual practice for sellers to _____ a Sales Contract as soon as a transaction is confirmed by them.
A. made out   B. draw up   C. make up   D. drafting

(   ) 7. As sheep wool is in great _____, we don't usually grant any discount _____ you could place an order for more than US $5,000.
A. demand . . . unless   B. requirement . . . expect
C. needs . . . until   D. wants . . . as long as

(   ) 8. Our buyers look forward to _____ their orders as soon as possible.
A. you accepting   B. the acceptance
C. your acceptance   D. your accepting

国际商务英语函电

(   ) 9. Immediately upon _____ the accepted draft we will arrange to ship the goods.

      A. receiving   B. receipt   C. receive   D. received

(   ) 10. While appreciating your difficulty in opening L/C, we regret _____ to accept D/P terms for this class of merchandise.

      A. to unable   B. not to able

      C. being not able   D. being unable

Task 3: Fill in the blanks with the words given and change the form when necessary.

| rule | documentary | appreciate | accommodation | acceptance |
| exception | draw | trial | precedent | due |

Dear Sirs,

We have received your letter of 15 Dec., and _____1_____ your intention to push the sales of our carpet in your country.

We regret we are unable to consider your request for payment on D/A terms, as a _____2_____, we ask for payment by L/C.

In view of our friendly relations, we will, as an _____3_____ case, accept payment for your trial order on D/P basis. In other words, we will _____4_____ on you by _____5_____ draft at sight, through our bank on collection basis, without L/C. But let us make it clear that this _____6_____ only for your _____7_____ order, which will in no case set a _____8_____.

We hope the above payment terms will be of _____9_____ to you and expect to receive your trial order in _____10_____ course.

Yours truly,

×××

Task 4: Translate the following sentences into Chinese.

1. Your request for payment by D/P has been taken into consideration. In view of the small amount of this transaction we are prepared to effect shipment on this basis.

_____

国际商务英语函电

2. Since our terms of payment are acceptable to other buyers, we trust you will agree to do business with us on these terms.

_____

3. As a special accommodation, we shall consider accepting payment by D/P during this sales-pushing stage.

_____

4. We propose to pay by bill of exchange at 30 d/s, documents against acceptance. Please confirm if this is acceptable to you.

_____

5. We are drawing on you at 60 days in favor of the Bank of China and trust you will meet our draft upon presentation.

_____

Task 5: Translate the following sentences into English.

1. 根据双方同意的条款,我们已向贵方开出随附发票所示金额的见票三十天付款的汇票。

_____

2. 请问你方今后是否愿意按承兑交单六十天付款条件卖货给我们? 你处其他供货人已按此条件向我方发货。

_____

3. 鉴于此笔交易额小,我们欲同意以即期付款交单方式支付货款。

_____

4. 按你方要求,我方破例接受承兑交单的付款方式,但只此一次,下不为例。

_____

5. 兹收到你方 2,100 美元的汇款。

_____

Task 6: Translate the following letter into English.

敬启者:

真空吸尘器

兹收到你方 12 月 19 日函,并感谢你方在贵国推销我方真空吸尘器的愿望。

国际商务英语函电

很抱歉我方不能考虑你方采用承兑交单付款方式支付的请求，通常我方只要求使用信用证付款。

鉴于我们的友好关系，我方破例接受你方试订订单采用付款交单方式，换言之，我方向你方开出即期跟单汇票，通过银行托收，不使用信用证。但是，我们还得说明这一照顾只适用于你方试订订单，下不为例。我们希望上述付款条件能为你方所接受，并期待能如期收到你方试订订单。

盼早复。

Knowledge Consolidation 知识点巩固

国际贸易货款的支付主要涉及支付工具、支付时间、支付地点和信用等方面。支付方式多种多样，汇付、托收和信用证是目前采用最多的三种方式。

汇付是付款人通过银行把款项汇给收款人的支付方式。汇付主要包括电汇、信汇和票汇三种方式。

托收是由卖方开具汇票，委托所在地银行，通过买方当地银行向买方收款。托收分光票托收和跟单托收两种。

信用证是银行根据进口商的请求，开给出口商的一种保证付款的书面凭证。信用证是国际贸易中使用最普遍的支付方式，它属于银行信用，因此对买卖双方来说，既可靠又安全。

李娜利用休息时间找了一些建议付款方式和回复付款要求的信函写作技巧及常用句型，以备将来可用，整理如下：

I. Writing skills.

1. When mentioning payment，plan your letters as follows：

（1）Mention the contract，goods，etc.

（2）Suggest the terms of payment and most importantly your reasons.

国际商务英语函电

（3）Wish the reader to accept.

2. Replies to payment：

（1）State that you have received his letter.

（2）Give your reply of agreeing or refusing and most importantly your reasons.

（3）State your goodwill and your wish to do the business with the reader.

II. Useful sentence patterns.

1. In view of the amount of this transaction being very small，we are prepared to accept payment by D/P at sight for the value of the goods shipped.

2. In compliance with your request we exceptionally accept delivery against D/P at sight，but this should not be regarded as a precedent.

3. We propose to pay by Bill of Exchange at 30 d/s，documents against acceptance.

4. As to payment，we are agreeable to draw on you at 60 days' sight，documents against acceptance.

5. The buyer shall pay 100% of the sales proceeds in advance by T/T to reach the seller not later than October 10，2012.

6. We enclose our cheque for USD 30,000 in settlement of your Invoice No. 230 of 20 April.

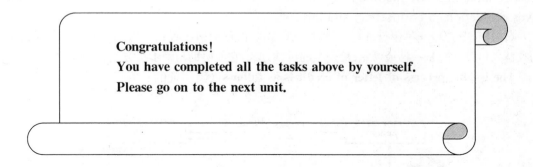

Congratulations！
You have completed all the tasks above by yourself.
Please go on to the next unit.

国际商务英语函电

Unit 8 Letter of Credit

Situational Introduction 情景介绍

　　如上一单元所述，信用证是目前对外贸易中最常用的付款方式。在李娜实习的第二个月，她的带教老师张先生就信用证的有关知识和使用方法为她做了一次专门的培训。

Knowledge to Impart 知识传授

Mr. Zhang: A letter of credit is a bank payment arrangement where the bank undertakes to pay the letter of credit's **beneficiary** upon presentation of acceptable **documents**. It is the most reliable and safe method of payment and it helps the trade with unknown buyers and gives protection to both sellers and buyers.

　　（信用证是一种通过银行进行的付款方式，凭此银行承担在收到恰当的文书材料时向信用证的收益人付款。它是一种最可靠、最安全的付款方式，它能协助与陌生买方交易并保护买卖双方）

The issuing process of letter of credit is as follows：（信用证的开立过程如下）

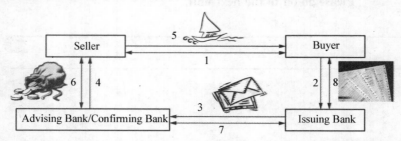

　　1. The seller and the buyer sign the sales contract.（买卖双方签订销售合同）

　　2. The buyer applies to issue a letter of credit.（买方申请开立信用证）

　　3. The issuing bank sends the letter of credit to the advising bank for checking.（开证行发信用证到通知行以供验证）

　　4. The advising bank advises the seller of its receipt of L/C.（通知行告知卖方已收到信用证）

　　5. The seller ships the merchandise to the buyer.（卖方发货）

　　6. The seller is paid upon presenting the required documents to the advising bank.（卖方提交材料，从通知行处得到货款）

　　7. The issuing bank pays the advising bank upon receipt of the documents.（开证行收

到材料后将货款付给通知行）

8. The issuing bank gets reimbursement from the buyer by presenting the documents. （开证行提交给买方单据以得到补偿）

Mr. Zhang: Here let us have a look at a sample letter of credit to have a general idea about it.

Canadian Commercial Bank
Irrevocable Credit No. 1234
International Trade Center
100 Main Street
Toronto，Ontario, Canada L1L1L1
December 15，2012

To：Outback Exporters Pty. Ltd.
    2200 Koala Drive
    Sydney，NSW 2000，Australia
                Advised through Australian Commercial bank，Sydney

Dear Sirs，

We hereby establish an irrevocable letter of credit in your favor for account of Better Importers limited，100 Polar Bear Avenue，Toronto，Ontario，Canada，for a sum not exceeding a total of USD 109，865. 20 （one hundred nine thousand eight hundred sixty-five and 20/100 United States dollars) and available by your draft drawn on us at sight for 100% of the invoice value，accompanied by the following documents：
    — Full set of Clean on Board Marine Bills of Lading to Shipper's Order，also marked "Freight Prepaid" and dated not later than 1 February，2013.
    — Commercial Invoice in triplicate.
    — Marine Insurance Policy or Certificate，in duplicate，covering all risks and war risk until warehouse destination，for at least 110% invoice value，in negotiable form with loss payable in Canada.
    — Certificate of Origin.

Evidencing shipment of：
    10，000 'Sure Look' Sunglasses，packed in boxes of 100
From Sydney，Australia to Toronto，Canada

Partial shipment is permitted.
Transhipment is permitted.

国际商务英语函电

This credit is valid in Sydney until February 15, 2013.

We hereby undertake to honor drafts drawn in accordance with the terms of the above credit. The amount and date of each negotiation must be endorsed on the back hereof by the negotiating bank which is to forward all documents to us by first and second airmails.

Yours faithfully,
CANADIAN COMMERCIAL BANK

Mr. Zhang: Li Na, please read it carefully and find out information about:

Required documents:_____

Description of shipment:_____

Terms of shipment:_____

Special conditions:_____

Li Na: OK.

请帮助李娜一起完成这个任务。

Mr. Zhang: Also you need to remember that a letter of credit should include the following:

- The name and addresses are complete and spelled correctly (开证行的名称、地址等应完整、拼写正确);
- The amount is sufficient to cover the shipment (钱款额度必须足够);
- The quantity is correct (商品数量正确);
- The unit price of goods, if stated in the L/C, conforms to the contract price (信用证中提及的商品单价必须与合同价格一致);
- The latest date of shipment or the shipping date is sufficient to dispatch the shipment (最迟装运期能保证商品及时运出);
- The port of shipment and the port of destination is correct (出发港口和到达港口必须正确);
- The type of risk and the amount of insurance coverage are stated, if required (如需要,在信用证中说明风险种类和保险金额).

More importantly is to know how to write a letter concerning L/C by using proper language. Next we are going to learn three types of this letter and please grasp some useful sentence patterns afterwards.

Letter 1: Urging Establishment of L/C (催开信用证)

Dear Sirs,

With reference to the 4,000 dozen shirts under our Sales Confirmation No. TE 151, we wish to draw your attention to the fact that the date of delivery is approaching, but up to present we have not received the Covering Letter of Credit. Please do your utmost to expedite its establishment, so that we may execute the order within the prescribed time.

In order to avoid subsequent amendment, please see to it that the L/C stipulations are in exact accordance with the terms of the contract.

We look forward to receiving your favorable response at an early date.

Yours faithfully,

×××

Letter 2: Asking for Amendment to L/C (要求修改信用证)

Dear Sirs,

While we thank you for your L/C No. 200345 issued by the ABC Bank, we regret to say that we have found some discrepancies after examining it carefully. You are, therefore, requested to make the following amendments:

1. The amount both in figures and in words should respectively read "GBP 14,750 (Say British Pounds Fourteen Thousand Seven Hundred and Fifty Only)";
2. "From Copenhagen to China port" should read "From China port to Copenhagen";
3. The Bill of Lading should be marked "Freight Prepaid" instead of "Freight Collect";
4. Delete the clause "Partial shipment and transhipment prohibited";
5. Insert the word "about" before the quantity.

As our goods have been ready for shipment for quite some time, please make the necessary amendment as soon as possible.

Yours Sincerely,

×××

国际商务英语函电

Letter 3: Reply to Letter Asking for Amendment to L/C（回复修改信用证的要求）

Dear Sirs，

We have received your letter dated June 3 and have to apologize to you for the mistake we've made in the above-mentioned L/C, which is completely due to carelessness.

We have already instructed our bank to amend the relevant L/C by cable without the least delay and we are sure the cable amendment will reach you in one or two days. As we are badly in need of the goods，we should be very grateful if you would kindly arrange prompt shipment.

Again，sorry for the mistake and thank you for your kind cooperation in this respect.

Yours faithfully，

× × ×

Mr. Zhang： Li Na，please find out the useful words and expressions from the above three letters.

Li NA： OK，but it will take some time.

Mr. Zhang： No problem. We will come back after the coffee break.

 Comments & Suggestions 评价及建议

李娜学习了以上三封信函,现在要求她熟练掌握以下单词与词组。

1. undertake [ˌʌndəˈteɪk] v. 承担，着手做;同意,答应
2. beneficiary [ˌbenɪˈfɪʃərɪ] n. 受益人,受惠者
3. reliable [rɪˈlaɪəbl] a. 可信赖的;可靠的;确实的
4. issue [ˈɪʃuː] v. 发行
5. exceed [ɪkˈsiːd] v. 超过;胜过
6. triplicate [ˈtrɪplɪkɪt] a. 一式三份的
7. duplicate [ˈdjuːplɪkɪt] a. 一式两份的
8. negotiable [nɪˈɡəʊʃɪəbl] a. 可协商

9. honor [ˈɒnə] v. 承兑,支付;允准;实践的
10. endorse [ɪnˈdɔːs] v. 在(发票、票据等)背面签名,背书
11. sufficient [səˈfɪʃənt] a. 足够的,充分的
12. dispatch [dɪˈspætʃ] v. 派遣;发送;快递
13. expedite [ˈekspɪdaɪt] v. 迅速执行;促进
14. discrepancy [dɪsˈkrepənsɪ] n. 不一致,不符,差异

国际商务英语函电

15. amend [ə'mend] *v.* 修改
16. read [ri:d] *v.* 读起来，写明
17. presentation [ˌprezən'teɪʃən] *n.* 陈述；报告；介绍；赠送
18. hereby [hɪə'baɪ] *adv.* 以此方式，特此
19. establish [ɪ'stæblɪʃ] *v.* 建立，创建
20. exceed [ɪk'si:d] *v.* 超过；超越
21. partial ['pɑ:ʃəl] *a.* 部分的

• •

1. draw on(upon) 开立
2. certificate of origin 原产地证明书
3. with reference to 关于
4. up to 直到(现在)
5. do one's utmost 尽某人最大努力
6. in accordance with 与……一致
7. bill of lading 提单
8. due to 由于
9. by cable 用电报发出
10. freight prepaid 运费预付

At the end of the workshop, Mr. Zhang helps Li Na to wrap up what has been covered today.
（培训结束后，张先生帮助李娜总结了今天学习的内容）

The process of issuing an L/C starts with the buyer. The buyer instructs his bank to issue an L/C in favor of the seller for the amount of the purchase. The buyer's bank (the opening bank) send the L/C to its correspondent bank (the notifying bank) in the seller's country, giving instruction about the amount of the credit, the beneficiary, the currency, the documents required and other special instructions. On its arrival, the correspondent bank advises the seller of the receipt of letter of credit.

Li Na is given the following exercises to consolidate the knowledge of L/C.
（要巩固信用证的知识，需要认真完成以下练习哦）

 Practice 小练习

Task 1: Fill in the blanks by choosing the appropriate word from the brackets.
1. We are glad that through our _____ efforts and cooperation at the Autumn Fair, the deal for 31 metric tons of Chinese Mild Steel Bars has been brought to a conclusion. (own, mutual)
2. Collection means that the exporter draws a draft according to the invoice and then instructs the bank to collect the amount of money _____ from the importer. (in the question, in question)
3. We presume your Bank, the United Malayan Banking Corporation, must have _____ with the Bank of China there and, if so, L/C arrangement can be easily made in Hong Kong. (connections, coincidence)

4. If the amount _____ that figure, payment by Letter of Credit will be required. (exceeds, overtakes)

5. The final result of business activities is to get the _____ amount of money for goods _____ or services rendered. (hinder, supplied)

6. Then the bank (remitting bank) instructs its correspondent bank (paying bank) to pay money to the _____. (recipience, recipient)

7. The letter of credit is an important method of _____ in international trade. (payment, concluding a contract)

8. When we checked the L/C with the _____ contract, we found that the amount in your L/C is insufficient. (relevant, regarding)

Task 2: Fill in the following blanks with the words or expressions in the boxes.

classified	complicated	mode	documents
signed	acceptance	namely	collection
presented	quantity	exporter	importers
stipulations	being	receipt	

Modes of Payment

Payment is an important part during the period of fulfilling the contract as well as in business negotiations. After a contract is ____1____, what the buyer will have to do is to make payment of the goods so as to get the ____2____ to take delivery.

Nowadays, in international trade, the most widely used ____3____ of payment is letter of credit (L/C), sight L/C or term L/C. Besides, there are two other modes, ____4____ Remittance and Collection. Remittance is ____5____ into three kinds, i. e. Mail Transfer (M/T), Demand Draft (D/D) and Telegraphic Transfer (T/T). There are two kinds of ____6____: Documents against Payment (D/P) and Documents against ____7____ (D/A).

However, payment is something quite ____8____ in business.

In foreign trade, payment is usually effected through a bank, as an L/C makes business with unknown ____9____ easy and provides protection to both the exporter and the importer. Simply speaking, the opening of an L/C means the relative bank agrees to pay the ____10____, so long as the documents ____11____ by the exporter appear to be in exact accordance with the L/C.

Upon ____12____ of the L/C, the exporter must examine it very carefully, especially the expiry date, the date of shipment, the amount, the ____13____ to be shipped, the documents required, etc., in order to make sure that the ____14____ in the L/C strictly conform to the contract. Any of them ____15____ not in order, the exporter should ask the importer for an amendment with the least possible delay.

Task 3: Cotton Weavers Ltd. has purchased 2,000 pieces of Cotton Print for delivery in December. As the goods have been ready for shipment for a long time, write a letter to the buyer urging him to establish the covering L/C immediately.

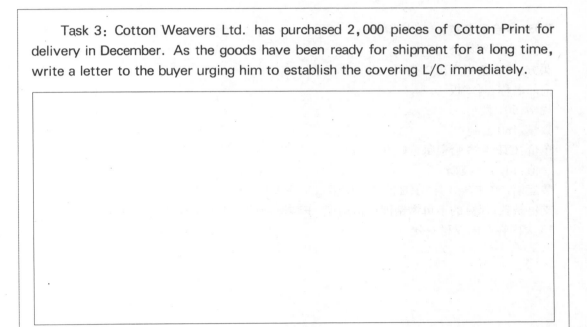

Task 4: Write a letter in English asking for amendment to the following letter of credit by checking it with the given contract terms.

Copenhagen Bank

Date: 4 January, 2011

To: Bank of China, Beijing

We hereby open our Irrevocable Transferable Letter of Credit No. 112235 in favor of Copenhagen Import Company for account of China Trading Corporation up to an amount of £1,455.00 (Say Pounds Sterling One Thousand Four Hundred and Fifty-five Only) for 100% of the invoice value relative to the shipment of:

150 metric tons of Writing Paper Type 501 as per S/C No. PO5476

From Copenhagen to China Port

Drafts to be drawn at sight on our bank and accompanied by the following documents marked "X"

...

Partial shipment and transhipment are prohibited.

Shipment must be effected not later than 31 March, 2011.

This L/C is valid at our counter until 15 April, 2011.

国际商务英语函电

PO5476 合同条款：

卖方：中国贸易公司

买方：哥本哈根进出口公司

商品名称：写字板

规格：501 型

数量：150 公吨

单价：CIF 哥本哈根每公吨 97 英磅

总值：14,550 英磅

装运期：2011 年 3 月 31 日前自中国港口至哥本哈根

支付条款：保兑的不可撤销即期信用证，于装运期前 1 个月开给卖方并于上述装运期后 15 天内在中国议付有效

Task 5：Put the following from English into Chinese or vice versa.

1. payment in advance _____
2. collection _____
3. credit standing _____
4. direct steamer _____
5. pay in installments _____
6. mail transfer _____
7. sight draft _____
8. cash against documents _____
9. documentary L/C _____
10. consular invoice _____

11. 电汇 _____
12. 票汇 _____
13. 不可撤销信用证 _____
14. 出票人 _____
15. 承兑交单 _____
16. 汇票 _____
17. 分批装运 _____
18. 即期付款交单 _____
19. 议付 _____
20. 付款人 _____

国际商务英语函电

Task 6: Choose the best answer to complete each of the following sentences.

(   ) 1. _____ the stipulations of S/C No. 167, you are to open the relative L/C before the end of November.

    A. According   B. Per

    C. In compliance with   D. Depending on

(   ) 2. You must be responsible for all the losses _____ from your delay in opening the covering L/C.

    A. rising   B. arising

    C. arousing   D. raising

(   ) 3. Our bank will accept your 60 days' draft _____ them for the amount of your invoice value.

    A. for   B. to   C. on   D. with

(   ) 4. Please amend L/C No. 283 to read "The L/C will _____ on February 28, 2010 in Singapore".

    A. expire   B. valid

    C. due to time   D. due

(   ) 5. We are glad to inform you that the L/C is now _____ the way to you.

    A. on   B. in   C. starting   D. setting of

(   ) 6. As the goods are ready for shipment, we _____ your L/C to be opened immediately.

    A. hope   B. anticipate

    C. await   D. expect

(   ) 7. Please extend your two relative _____ for 15 days.

    A. letter of credits   B. letters of credit

    C. L/Cs   D. L/C

(   ) 8. Attached to this letter _____ a copy of B/L, along with copies of invoice and weight memo.

    A. are   B. is   C. have been   D. /

(   ) 9. It is important that your client _____ the relative L/C not later than May 12, 2011.

    A. must open   B. has to open

    C. open   D. opens

(   ) 10. We invite your attention to the fact _____ the L/C covering your order No. 501 has not reached us in spite of our repeated request.

    A. what   B. that   C. where   D. which

国际商务英语函电

Knowledge Consolidation 知识点巩固

李娜利用休息时间找了一些与开立信用证有关的常用句型和注意事项，以备将来可用，整理如下：

I. Useful sentence patterns.

1. In view of our long business relation, we will make an exception to our rules and accept L/C at 30 days (after sight).

2. Payment is to be made against sight draft drawn under a confirmed, irrevocable letter of credit without recourse for the full amount of purchase.

3. We hope that you will take your commercial reputation in all seriousness and open the L/C at once, otherwise you will be responsible for all the losses arising from your failure to do so.

4. Much to our regret, we have not yet received your letter of credit against our Sales Confirmation No. 2345, although it should have reached us by the end of May, as stipulated.

5. According to the stipulations in our Sales Confirmation No. 315, you should send us your letter of credit one month preceding the date of shipment.

6. On examination, we find that the amount of your L/C is insufficient. Please increase the unit price from USD $5.6 to USD $6.5 and the total amount to USD $32,500.

7. The shipment date is approaching. It would be advisable for you to open the L/C covering your order No. 345 as early as possible so as to enable us to effect shipment within the stipulated time limit.

8. Please amend (adjust) L/C No. 321 as follows:

(1) Amount is to be increased up to US $21,340.

(2) Validity is to be extended to October 30.

(3) The words "Transhipment Not Allowed" are to be deleted.

II. In using L/C, exporters should pay attention to the following things.

1. When the L/C has arrived, the clerk should make a point of checking the L/C terms with the contract stipulations to the letter, and should not let even a minute point escape his attention.

2. There may be circumstances where the buyer fails to establish the letter of credit, or the letter of credit does not reach the seller in time, then a letter, usually a fax or a telex has to be sent to the buyer to urge him to expedite the L/C or to ascertain its whereabouts (查明下落).

3. On the basis of Statement One above, if the clerk finds differences between the L/C and the contract, or some unforeseen special clauses to which the seller does not agree, the seller should send an advice to the buyer, asking him to make

amendments. The buyer can likewise ask for amendments if he finds something in the L/C needs to be altered.

4. Sometimes the seller may fail to get the goods ready for shipment in time or the buyer may request that the shipment be postponed for one reason or another，then the seller will have to ask for extension of the expiry date as well as the date of shipment of the L/C. In addition，in order to leave sufficient time to the seller to make out the shipping documents and the banks to make their negotiation，the date of shipment and the expiry date of the L/C should be made at least two weeks apart.

Task：Choose the best ones to well translate the given sentences.

（　）1. 因为下月无直达船驶往你港，请将信用证修改为"允许转船"。
   A. As no direct steamer to your port next month，we have to request you to amend the L/C to read "Transhipment Allowed".
   B. Owing to there is no direct steamer sailing for your port next month，please amend the L/C to read "Transhipment Allowed".
   C. As there is no direct steamer sailing for your port next month，please amend the L/C to read "Transhipment Allowed".
   D. Owing to no direct steamer to your port next month，we have to ask you to amending the L/C to read "Transhipment Allowed".

（　）2. 务请于下月初开出信用证，并允许分批装运和转船。
   A. Please pay attention to open the L/C at the beginning of next month，allow transhipment and partial shipment.
   B. Please see to open the L/C at the beginning of next month，to allow transhipment and partial shipment.
   C. Please see to it that the L/C is opened at the beginning of next month，allowing transhipment and partial shipment.
   D. Please draw your attention to the fact that the L/C established at the beginning of next month，allowing transhipment and partial shipment.

（　）3. 请速开证，以便准时装运。
   A. Please rush your L/C，thus making possible to effect timely shipment.
   B. Please expedite your L/C，so that shipment on time.
   C. Please open the L/C as soon as possible，so as to enable us to effect shipment on time.
   D. Please urge your L/C establishment，so as shipment is on time.

（　）4. 若交易总额在 USD 1,000,000 以上，必须用信用证。
   A. If the amount exceeds USD 1,000,000，an L/C is required.
   B. If the amount exceed USD 1,000,000，an L/C is required.
   C. Should the amount is up to USD 1,000,000，an L/C is required.
   D. Should the amount be exceed USD 1,000,000，an L/C is required.

国际商务英语函电

Congratulations!

You have completed all the tasks above by yourself.

Please go on to the next unit.

Unit 9　Packing

Situational Introduction 情景介绍

　　今天,李娜身着一套漂亮的衣服来到实习公司上班,带教老师张先生见后先赞美了一番,然后引申说到货物的包装。如何使货物的外表既美观又能符合客户的要求呢? 张先生向李娜讲解了有关货物包装的知识以及如何书写有关货物包装的商务信函。

Knowledge to Impart 知识传授

Mr. Zhang: Good morning，Li Na. Oh，you are dressed so beautifully today!

Li Na: Good morning，Mr. Zhang. Thank you. I just wear a new suit.

Mr. Zhang: Clothes are really important to people. They not only make us beautiful，but also make us protected from coldness. Li Na，do you know that goods also need clothes in international business?

Li Na: Do you mean packing?

Mr. Zhang: Yes，quite right. Today I will tell you something about packing in the business world，and you should be good at understanding and writing the business letters on packing.

Li Na: Thank you.

Mr. Zhang: You know，dressing is an art，especially for women，and packing is also an art that businessmen must learn to grasp. The real art of packing is to get the contents into a nice and compact shape. All the buyers expect that their goods will reach them in perfect conditions.

Li Na: I think packing is of particular importance in foreign trade.

Mr. Zhang: Yes，sure，because goods travel long distances before reaching their destinations，often across oceans or across continents. Accidents，rough weather，unloading and reloading on the way，everything has to be taken into consideration.

Li Na: Is there a special department for export packing in large companies? Why?

Mr. Zhang: Well，nearly all the large export firms have established a special department for export packing，and the whole question is under regular review. New packing materials are being developed，which are light and strong，and new methods are being found to ensure the safe transport of goods. Many firms employ a specialist export packer or forwarding agent to do packing for them. Because the buyer has the right to expect that his goods will reach him in perfect condition, the seller has to get the goods into a nice, compact shape that will stay the way during the rough journey. Nothing is more infuriating to a buyer than to find his goods damaged or part missing on arrival; and nothing is more likely to lose a customer than this.

Li Na: Which is more important, to make the goods secure or to make the goods beautiful?

Mr. Zhang: The general plan in all packing is to make the goods secure for journey, and to keep the package as small and light as possible, because freight is also an important factor to be kept in mind.

Li Na: How many types of packing are there?

Mr. Zhang: Well, packing can generally be divided into two types: outer packing and inner packing. Outer packing is used for the convenience of protecting and transporting goods. Inner packing, also known as small packing, is designed for the promotion of sales.

Li Na: What are the most commonly-used packing containers?

Mr. Zhang: Packing varies with the nature of the contents. The most commonly-used packing containers are cartons, cases, crates, drums, barrels, bales, tins, and carboys.

Li Na: Thank you for telling me so much, Mr. Zhang!

Mr. Zhang: You are welcome!

Li Na: Mr. Zhang, would you please show me some example letters on packing?

Mr. Zhang: No problem. Here is a letter on the buyer's requirement for packing, please study it and try to write an reply letter to it.

Dear Li Na,

We have received your letter dated November 12, enclosing the sales confirmation in duplicate, but we wish to state that after going through the contract we find that the packing clause in it is not clear enough. The relative clause reads as follows:

Packing: Each piece in a plastic bag, 20 small poly-bags in a craft paper bag, 2 craft paper bags to a carton.

In order to eliminate possible future troubles, we would like to make clear beforehand our packing requirements as follows:

All garments we ordered should be packed in international standard carton, each piece in a plastic bag, 20 small poly-bags in a craft paper bag, 2 craft paper bags to a carton. In addition, please make sure that they should be packed in seaworthy wooden cases in transit.

国际商务英语函电

As for the outer packing, please mark the port of destination and our order number in stencil ink of high quality. Furthermore, such indicative marks as KEEP DRY, INFLAMMABLE should also be indicated.

Look forward to your early reply.

Yours sincerely,
John Strong

阅完来信,李娜书写了一封复函,现在她请张先生帮忙看看这封信是否有不足之处。

Li Na: Mr. Zhang, I've read the example letter and written one to answer it, would you please give me some advice?

Mr. Zhang: Good, let me read it first. ... Oh, Li Na, well done! Just correct some mistakes, and it will be a good business letter. I think the correct one should be like this:

Dear Mr. Strong,

We thank you for your letter on the packing requirements, and we have pleasure in informing you that we accept them.

All types of ladies' woolen knitted garments, men's garments and kids' wear you ordered have been ready. Since packing not only serves as a form of protection, but also facilitates loading, unloading and stowage, prevents pilferage, and promotes sales, we have to pay special attention to it.

As garments is moisture absorbent especially in hot rainy weather, just as you requested, we packed the garments in craft paper bags containing 20 small poly-bags, two craft paper bags to one carton lined with waterproof paper. In consideration of the nature of the goods that are susceptible to dampness, we make sure that they have been all packed in seaworthy wooden cases in transit.

As for the outer packing, the port of destination and your order number were marked, and such indicative marks as KEEP DRY, INFLAMMABLE were also indicated.

Yours faithfully,
Li Na

Li Na: That's better. Thank you, Mr. Zhang.

国际商务英语函电

Mr. Zhang: It's my pleasure. Now I would like you to do more practice according to what we have talked about.

Li Na: Let me try.

 Practice·小练习

Task 1: Answer the following questions.

1. Why is packing of particular importance in foreign trade?

   _____

2. Why must the seller get the goods into a nice, compact shape during the journey?

   _____

3. Why have large export firms established a special department for export packing?

   _____

4. How are the new packing materials?

   _____

5. What are the most commonly-used packing containers?

   _____

6. What's the real art of packing?

   _____

7. If a buyer finds his goods damaged or part missing on arrival, what will happen?

   _____

8. Is freight also an important factor to be kept in mind?

   _____

9. Generally, how many types of packing are there? What are they?

   _____

10. What is inner packing designed for?

    _____

Task 2: Decide whether the following statements are true or false.

(   ) 1. Outer packing is used for the promotion of sales.

(   ) 2. Nearly all the large export firms have established a special department for export packing.

(   ) 3. The general plan in all packing is to make the goods beautiful.

(   ) 4. All the buyers expect that their goods will reach them in perfect conditions.

(   ) 5. Packing varies with the nature of the contents.

Task 3: Choose the right answer for each sentence.

(   ) 1. The general plan in all packing is to make the goods _____ for journey.

        A. to secure   B. securing   C. secured   D. secure

(   ) 2. Freight is also an important factor _____.

        A. to be kept in mind   B. be kept in mind

        C. to keep in mind   D. keep in mind

(   ) 3. Packing _____ the nature of the contents.

        A. varies as   B. varies along   C. varies with   D. varies about

(   ) 4. _____ is more infuriating to a buyer _____ to find his goods damaged or part missing on arrival.

        A. None... like   B. Anybody... likely

        C. Anything... as   D. Nothing... than

(   ) 5. Packing is _____ in foreign trade.

        A. of particular important   B. of particular importance

        C. of particularly important   D. particularly importance

(   ) 6. We regret that we have suffered heavy loss _____ your improper packing.

        A. resulted from   B. resulted in

        C. resulting from   D. resulting in

(   ) 7. We would suggest that you _____ the carton with double straps.

        A. secure   B. will secure   C. securing   D. are secured

(   ) 8. The adoption of containers facilitated _____ to a great tent.

        A. to load and unload   B. loading and unloading

        C. load and unload   D. loaded and unloaded

(   ) 9. Packing: Each piece _____ a plastic bag, 20 small poly-bags _____ a craft paper bag, 2 craft paper bags to a carton.

        A. in... in   B. to... to   C. in... to   D. to... in

(   ) 10. It is essential that the goods must _____ packed in strong wooden cases.

        A. will be   B. be   C. are   D. to be

Task 4: Translation Work.

A. Please put the following into English.

1. 有关包装要求的信函_____

2. 为了消除将来可能出现的麻烦_____

3. 包装条款_____

4. 考虑到这批货的质地_____

5. 用适于航海的木箱包装_____

国际商务英语函电

B. Translate the following into Chinese.

1. the commonly-used packing containers _____

2. outer packing and inner packing _____

3. travel long distances before reaching their destinations _____

4. special department for export packing _____

5. during the rough journey _____

C. Translate the following business letter into Chinese, then write a letter to reply to it.

China National Import & Export Corp.
Shanghai
China

Dear Sirs,

A shipment of ready-made garments has arrived on May 10th. Having examined the goods thoroughly, we venture to say that the packing needs improvement. For instance, the cartons used are not strong enough to protect the contents from getting damaged during transit. We have enquired of some of our clients about the packing in question. They say:

1. Such cartons are easy to cut open because the cardboard of which the cartons are made is rather thin, thus making pilferage become possible.

2. If and when goods are to be transported at a certain port, the cartons will stand in the open on the wharf and, in heavy rains, be subjected to damage as the cartons will surely be soaked.

3. During loading and unloading, the cartons are to be piled up, hence breakage is unavoidable because the cartons are too thin to stand heavy pressure.

4. The insurance companies, on knowing this, will shift their responsibilities to the goods being packed in cartons not fit for ocean transport and refuse compensation for losses.

From the above comments, you can readily see that our clients are justified in their anxieties over your packing. As far as packing is concerned, they prefer wooden cases to cartons for future shipments.

We sincerely hope that you will take this matter into consideration and make necessary improvements so as to avoid unforeseen troubles arising from faulty packing. Your early response will be much appreciated.

Yours sincerely,
B. T. Greenwood Co.
Manager

You may write the reply letter here.

Comments & Suggestions 评价及建议

李娜出色地完成了四项任务,现在要求她熟练掌握以下单词与词组。

1. dress [dres] v. (给……)穿衣
2. especially [ɪ'speʃəlɪ] adv. 特别,尤其
3. art [ɑːt] n. 艺术
4. grasp [grɑːsp] v. 掌握,领会,抓住
5. content ['kɒntent] n. 内容,容量
6. compact [kəm'pækt] a. 结实的
7. rough [rʌf] a. 粗糙的;崎岖不平的
8. shape [ʃeɪp] n. 外形,形状,形态
9. journey ['dʒɜːnɪ] n. 旅行,旅程
10. condition [kən'dɪʃən] n. 情况;状态
11. particular [pə'tɪkjʊlə] a. 值得注意的;特别的;不寻常的
12. destination [ˌdestɪ'neɪʃən] n. 目的地
13. load [ləʊd] v. 装载,装填,使担负
14. unload [ʌn'ləʊd] v. 卸货
15. reload [riː'ləʊd] v. 再装
16. department [dɪ'pɑːtmənt] n. 部,局,处
17. establish [ɪ'stæblɪʃ] v. 成立,建立
18. regular ['regjʊlə] a. 有规律的
19. review [rɪ'vjuː] n. 回顾;再检查
20. method ['meθəd] n. 方法;办法
21. ensure [ɪn'ʃʊə] v. 确保,保证
22. specialist ['speʃəlɪst] n. 专家,行家
23. infuriating [ɪn'fjʊərɪˌeɪtɪŋ] a. 令人发怒的
24. customer ['kʌstəmə] n. 消费者
25. secure [sɪ'kjʊə] v. 保护,使安全
26. freight [freɪt] n. 运费,货物,货运
27. convenience [kən'viːnjəns] n. 便利,方便
28. container [kən'teɪnə] n. 容器,集装箱
29. vary ['veərɪ] v. 变化
30. carton ['kɑːtən] n. 硬纸盒
31. case [keɪs] n. 箱,盒
32. crate [kreɪt] n. 板条
33. drum [drʌm] n. 鼓型圆桶箱
34. barrel ['bærəl] n. 桶
35. carboy ['kɑːbɔɪ] n. 玻璃瓶,钢瓶
36. beforehand [bɪ'fɔːˌhænd] adv. 预先,事先
37. stowage ['stəʊɪdʒ] n. 贮藏
38. pilferage ['pɪlfərɪdʒ] n. 偷盗
39. susceptible [sə'septəbl] a. 易受影响的

• •

1. be designed for 为……而设计
2. inner packing 内包装
3. outer packing 外包装
4. sales confirmation 成交确认书,销货确认,销售证明
5. international standard 国际标准
6. packing clause 包装条款
7. craft paper bag 牛皮纸袋
8. in addition 另外
9. seaworthy wooden case 适于航海的木箱
10. in transit 在路上,在途中
11. packing material 包装材料
12. forwarding agent 货运代理
13. in perfect condition 状况良好
14. be kept in mind 牢记在心
15. be divided into ... 被分为……
16. as small and light as possible 尽可能又小又轻
17. vary with ... 随着……的变化而变化

Knowledge Consolidation 知识点巩固

在张先生的指导下,李娜掌握了有关货物包装的基本知识并学会如何就有关内容与客户取得联系和沟通。但要确保书写一封好的商务信函,我们必须认真学习以下关键词组和句型。

I. Useful phrases.

1. be important to . . .   对……来说很重要

e. g. The document was very important to our company. 这个文件对我们公司很重要。

2. protected from coldness   防寒

3. be packed in iron drums   用金属鼓型圆桶包装

4. during the rough journey   在崎岖不平的路途中

5. of particular importance = particularly important

be + of + 名词结构,相当于其中名词所对应的形容词的意思,说明被修饰词具有某种特征或属性。

e. g. of no interest = not interesting

6. travel long distance   长途跋涉

7. have to be taken into consideration   必须纳入考虑范围之内

8. establish a special department for export packing   专门设立一个部门负责出口商品的包装

9. be under regular review   纳入常规检查之中

10. ensure the safe transport of goods   确保货物运输的安全

11. have the right to . . .   有权……

12. nothing is more infuriating than this   没有比这更令人愤怒的了

13. find goods damaged or part missing on arrival   在货物到达时发现货物受损或部分货物丢失

14. be more likely to do . . .   很可能会去做……

15. make the goods secure   使货物安全

16. as . . . as possible   尽可能……

e. g. keep the package as small and light as possible   使包裹尽可能又小又轻

17. promotion of sales   提高销售量,促进销售

e. g. be designed for the promotion of sales   为促销而设计的

18. the most commonly-used packing containers   最常用的包装容器

19. a letter on buyers' requirement for packing   关于买方包装要求的信函

20. in duplicate   一式两份
    in triplicate   一式三份

e. g. enclosing the sales confirmation in duplicate   附上销售确认书,一式两份

21. be packed in international standard carton   采用国际标准纸箱包装

22. as for . . .   至于……

23. in stencil ink of high quality   用高质量的金属模板或蜡纸版印刷

国际商务英语函电

24. in consideration of the nature of the goods 考虑到货物的质地

25. be susceptible to 对……敏感

e. g. be susceptible to dampness 容易吸收湿气

II. Useful sentence patterns.

1. The packing must be seaworthy. 包装应该适于航海。

2. Thank you for your letter of March 12, informing us of your clients' comments on our packing. 感谢您三月十二日的来信，让我们知道您的客户对我们包装的评价。

3. The cardboard used for making cartons is light but compact. It keeps down packing costs and helps customers save on freight. 用于制造纸板箱的纸板虽然轻但很牢固，能降低包装成本并帮助客户节约运费。

4. The real art of packing is to get the contents into a nice, compact shape. 包装的艺术就是使商品外观漂亮又结实。

5. We do not object to packing in cartons. 我们并不反对用纸板箱包装。

6. The packing inside the case was too loose. 箱内包装垫料太松。

7. The attached list will give you details. 详见所附清单。

8. Cases must be nailed tightly and secured by overall metal strapping. 箱子必须钉紧并用金属带或金属条全面加固。

9. In order to avoid the movement inside the cases, plastic moldings should be padded within the cases. 为了避免货物在箱内晃动，箱内必须填满塑料垫衬。

10. Cases must be numbered from 1 to 50, and the word FRAGILE must be stenciled clearly in normal size on all four sides of the container. 箱子从 1 到 50 按顺序编号，FRAGILE（易碎）字样按常规大小醒目地写在四周。

11. The packing of our men's shirts is each in a poly-bag, five dozens to a carton, lined with waterproof paper and bound with two straps outside. 我们的男衬衫包装为每件套一塑料袋，五打装一纸箱，内衬防潮纸，外打两道箱带。

12. Folding chairs are packed two pieces to a carton. 折叠椅每两把装一个纸板箱。

13. The peanuts should be packed in double gunny bags. 花生应该用双层麻袋包装。

14. The greatest care must be given to packing and crating as any damage in transit would cause us heavy losses. 必须给包装和装箱以极大关注，因为运输途中如出现货损会给我们带来巨大的损失。

15. The cases used for packing our goods must be light and strong. They should save shipping space and facilitate the stowage and distribution of the goods. 用于包装我们货物的箱子必须又轻又结实。它们应该能节省舱位并便于货物贮藏和分发。

16. When packing, please take into account that the boxes are likely to receive rough handling. 在包装的时候，应考虑到这些包装箱很可能会遭到粗暴搬运。

17. If you find any defect in our packing, please do not hesitate to let us know. 如果您发现我们的包装有什么纰漏，请毫不犹豫地告诉我们。

18. We think you will understand that our candid statement is made for our mutual benefit. 相信您能明白我们率直的语言都是为了我们双方的利益。

19. Packing is a sensitive subject which often leads to trade dispute. 包装是一个经常引起贸易争端的敏感话题。

20. Packing varies with the nature of the contents. 包装随着商品质地的不同而不同。

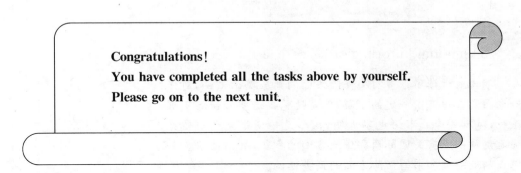

Congratulations!
You have completed all the tasks above by yourself.
Please go on to the next unit.

Unit 10　Insurance

Situational Introduction 情景介绍

　　李娜最近读了很多有关保险方面的商务英语信函,对保险方面的知识有了一定的了解,但是她觉得这些知识还不够系统,对有些专业术语也不太明白,于是她请张先生给她系统地讲解一下有关国际商务保险方面的知识,并向他请教如何正确地解读和书写保险方面的商务信函。

Knowledge to Impart 知识传授

Li Na：Good morning, Mr. Zhang.

Mr. Zhang：Good morning, Li Na.

Li Na：I'm sorry to bother you, but I really need your help in learning insurance in international trade.

Mr. Zhang：Well, I'm very glad to help you, and I have prepared some letters on business insurance for you to study.

Li Na：Thank you, Mr. Zhang.

Mr. Zhang：In international trade, goods are normally insured for full amount of their value to avoid all the possible risks, losses and damages during the process of the transport.

Li Na：Mr. Zhang, is insurance so necessary in international trade?

Mr. Zhang：Yes. Because goods travel long distances before reaching their destinations, often across oceans or across continents. Accidents, rough weather, unloading and reloading on the way, everything has to be taken into consideration in order to avoid all the possible risks, losses and damages.

Li Na：What's the purpose of taking out insurance?

Mr. Zhang：The purpose of insurance is to provide compensation for these who suffer from loss or damage. It's a contract of indemnity, which is generally made in the form of insurance policy.

Li Na：Mr. Zhang, who will arrange insurance, the buyer or the seller?

Mr. Zhang：Depending on the trade terms, insurance may be handled by the buyer or the seller, and the kinds of insurance vary with the modes of transports.

Li Na：How many types of marine cargo insurance are there?

Mr. Zhang：As far as foreign trade is concerned, there are various kinds of risks which can be covered under an insurance policy. The people's Insurance Company of China provides

three basic types:
- Free from Particular Average (F. P. A. 平安险);
- With Particular Average (W. P. A. 水渍险);
- All Risks (一切险).

Li Na: What are the rest?

Mr. Zhang: As far as I know, there are about 20 kinds of additional risks that you will likely see in the business letters:
- Theft, Pilferage & Non-delivery (T. P. N. D. 偷窃、提货不着险);
- Fresh and/or Rain Water Damage Risk(淡水雨淋险);
- Shortage Risk (短量险);
- Intermixture & Contamination Risk (混杂、玷污险);
- Leakage Risk (渗漏险);
- Clash & Breakage Risk (碰损破碎险);
- Taint of Odour Risk (串味险);
- Sweating & Heating Risk (受潮受热险);
- Hook Damage Risk (钩损险);
- Rust Risk (锈损险);
- Breakage of Packing Risk (包装破裂险);
- Strikes (罢工险);
- War Risk (战争险);
- Import Duty Risk (进口关税险);
- On Deck Risk (舱面险);
- Rejection Risk (拒收险);
- Failure to Delivery Risk (交货不到险);
- Survey in Customs Risk(海关检验险);
- Survey at Jetty Risk (码头检验险);
- Aflatoxin (黄曲霉素险).

Li Na: Thank you, Mr. Zhang. I will learn these terms by heart one by one, so that I can know them when I read business letters on insurance.

Mr. Zhang: That's good. You are really a hardworking girl.

Li Na: Mr. Zhang, would you please tell me the whole process of covering insurance?

Mr. Zhang: Yes, of course. The stages of arranging insurance cover are as follows:

A. The party seeking cover completes a proposal form.
B. The insurance company assesses the risk and fixes a premium to be paid.
C. The premium is paid and cover starts.
D. If a loss is suffered, the insured makes a claim for compensation to be paid.
E. The claim is investigated, and if found to be valid, the compensation is paid.

Li Na: I see, it's so concise, thank you.

Mr. Zhang: There are some important expressions on insurance that you should

国际商务英语函电

understand, such as the insurance policy, the insurance certificate, floating policy, open cover, cover note, the insurer, the insured and so on.

The **insurance policy** is the principal document and is in fact a contract of indemnity. As the insurance may cover a certain period of time or many shipments of goods, another document, the **insurance certificate** is used. The policy may be known as a **floating policy**, that is to say, it covers a large sum of money, and such a policy is represented by certificates for each separate consignment. There is also a procedure of insurance often used now, known as **open cover**, by which there is a rather general arrangement between the **insurer** and the **insured**, and the latter will have all consignments insured by the former. A **cover note** is a small document issued by the insurance agents to their customers, to tell them that their goods are insured, and to give proof of this until the policy is ready.

Li Na: Thank you, Mr. Zhang. May I have a look at the specimen letters on insurance prepared for me?

Mr. Zhang: OK, here you are. Please take these letters home and read them carefully. If you have any questions, just contact me.

Li Na: Many Thanks.

Mr. Zhang: You are welcome.

Example Letter 1

December 8, 2011
Global Insurance (Asia) Ltd.
5ᵗʰ Floor, 500 Xinshiji Blvd
Pudong, Shanghai

Ladies/Gentlemen,

We will be sending a consignment of 100 photocopiers to Daehan Trading Company, Limited, Pusan, the Republic of Korea. The consignment is to be loaded onto the S.S. Dashun which sails from Shanghai on December 16 and is due in Pusan on December 19.

Details with regard to packing and values are attached, and we would be grateful if you could quote a rate covering all risks from port to port.

As the matter is urgent, we would appreciate a prompt reply. Thank you.

Very truly yours,
Zhang Bonian

国际商务英语函电

Mr. Zhang Bonian
Export Manager
Cathy Business Machines Imp. & Exp. Corp.
Central Boulevard
Pudong，Shanghai

Dear Mr. Zhang，

Thank you for your fax of 8 December，in which you asked about cover for a shipment of photocopiers from Shanghai to Pusan.

I note from the details attached to your letter that the net amount of the invoice is USD 98,000.00 and payment is by letter of credit. I would therefore suggest a valued policy against all risks for which we can quote 0.0065.

We will issue a cover note as soon as you complete and return the enclosed declaration form.

Yours sincerely，
Daniel Cooke
Greater China Region

Encl：Declaration form

Dear Sir or Madam，

We thank you for your order of 23 October for 1,000 sets of Box Socket Sets，which is planned on CIF Basis.

In reply，we would like to inform you that most of our clients are placing their orders with us on CIF basis. This will save their time and simplify procedures. May we suggest that you would follow this practice?

For your information，we usually effect insurance with the People's Insurance Company of China for 110% of the invoice value. Our insurance company is a state-

国际商务英语函电

operated enterprise enjoying high prestige in setting claims promptly and has agents in all main ports and regions of the world. Should any damage occurs to the goods，you may file your claim with their agent at your end，who will take up the matter without delay.

We insure the goods against the usual risks and in the present case All Risks. Should broader coverage be required，the extra premium is for the buyer's account.

We hope you will agree to our suggestion and look forward to your favorable reply.

Yours faithfully，
John Strong

According to what Li Na has learned，she is required to do the following practice.
根据李娜所学到的知识，要求她完成以下练习。

 Practice 小练习

Task 1：Answer the following questions.

1. Are goods normally insured in international trade?
   _____

2. What may happen if goods travel long distances before reaching their destinations?
   _____

3. Why does everything have to be taken into consideration when the goods are on the way in international business?
   _____

4. What is the purpose of arranging insurance?
   _____

5. Is insurance a contract of indemnity?
   _____

6. Do the kinds of insurance vary with the modes of transports?
   _____

7. How many basic types of insurance does the People's Insurance Company of China provide?
   _____

8. How many stages are there to arrange insurance?
   _____

9. The insurance policy is the principal document，isn't it?
   _____

10. What is a cover note issued for?

_____

Task 2: Decide whether the following statements are true or false.

(   ) 1. The purpose of insurance is to provide compensation for these who suffer from loss or damage.

(   ) 2. In doing international business, it is the buyers who arrange insurance.

(   ) 3. As soon as the premium is paid, the cover starts.

(   ) 4. The People's Insurance Company of China provides about 20 basic types.

(   ) 5. The claim is investigated, and if found to be invalid, the compensation is paid.

Task 3: Choose the right answer for each sentence.

(   ) 1. Insurance is _____ risks.
     A. on   B. for   C. against   D. with

(   ) 2. The idea of insurance is to obtain indemnity _____ any happening that may cause loss of money.
     A. on the event of   B. in the event of
     C. on the case of   D. in the case of

(   ) 3. There is also a procedure of insurance often _____ now, known as open cover.
     A. use   B. uses   C. using   D. used

(   ) 4. The insurance company assesses the risk and fixes a premium _____.
     A. to be paid   B. to pay
     C. to have paid   D. is paid

(   ) 5. As the matter is urgent, we would _____ a prompt reply.
     A. appreciate   B. interest   C. worry   D. intend

(   ) 6. The extra premium _____ by us.
     A. is born   B. will be taken
     C. will be borne   D. will be undertaken

(   ) 7. If you desire to _____ your goods against All Risks, we can provide such coverage.
     A. guarantee   B. guard   C. cover   D. protect

(   ) 8. If a loss is suffered, the _____ makes a claim for compensation to be paid.
     A. insure   B. insuring   C. insurer   D. insured

国际商务英语函电

（　　）9. Details with regard to packing and values are attached，and we would be grateful if you could quote a rate _____ All Risks from port to port.

    A．covering   B．be covering

    C．to cover   D．to be covered

（　　）10. As the matter is urgent，we would _____ reply.

    A．appreciating a promptly   B．appreciate a prompt

    C．enjoy a short   D．provide a quick

Task 4：Translation work.

A. Please put the following into Chinese.

1. What risks is this insurance company able to cover?

_____

2. For the sake of safety，we recommend you to cover insurance for shipment against All Risks and War Risks.

_____

3. W. P. A. coverage is too narrow for the shipment of this nature. Please extend the coverage to include T. P. N. D.

_____

4. In the insurance business，the term "average" simply means "loss" in most cases.

_____

5. The purpose of insurance is to provide compensation for these who suffer from loss or damage.

_____

B. Please put the following into English.

1. 请填写一下投保单。

_____

2. 通常的保险金额为发票的110%。

_____

3. 综合险不包括拒收险。

_____

4. 你方报出的保险费率不符合我方的期望。

_____

5. 我们很高兴地通知您，我们已向中国人民保险公司为上述货物投保了战争险。

_____

Comments & Suggestions 评价及建议

李娜出色地完成了四项任务,现在要求她熟练掌握以下单词与词组。

1. insurance [ɪn'ʃʊərəns] *n*. 保险
2. bother ['bɒðə] *v*. 麻烦,打扰
3. consideration [kənˌsɪdə'reɪʃən] *n*. 考虑
4. avoid [ə'vɔɪd] *v*. 避免
5. valid ['vælɪd] *a*. 有效的
6. compensation [ˌkɒmpən'seɪʃən] *n*. 赔偿
7. indemnity [ɪn'demnɪtɪ] *n*. 赔偿
8. average ['ævərɪdʒ] *n*. 平均
9. investigate [ɪn'vestɪgeɪt] *v*. 调查
10. principal ['prɪnsəpəl] *a*. 首要的, 主要的
11. consignment [kən'saɪnmənt] *n*. 发货,委托
12. procedure [prə'siːdʒə] *n*. 程序, 手续
13. seek [siːk] *v*. 寻找,探求
14. assess [ə'ses] *v*. 评估
15. premium ['priːmɪəm] *n*. 保险费
16. proof [pruːf] *n*. 证据
17. cover ['kʌvə] *v*. 投保各种保险
18. attach [ə'tætʃ] *v*. 附上,贴上
19. declaration [ˌdeklə'reɪʃən] *n*. 申报

●●●●●●●●●●●●●●●●●●●●●●●●●●●●●●●●●●●●

1. reach the destination　到达目的地
2. rough weather　恶劣的天气
3. suffer from　忍受,遭受
4. contract of indemnity　赔偿契约, 赔偿合同
5. insurance policy　保险单
6. trade terms　贸易条款
7. mode of transport　运输模式
8. marine cargo insurance　海运货物保险
9. as far as　远到,直到,至于
10. basic type of risk　基本险
11. additional risk　附加险
12. proposal form　投保单
13. insurance certificate　保险凭证
14. floating policy　总保险单
15. open cover　预约保险单
16. cover note　暂保单
17. the insurer　保险者,保险公司
18. the insured　被保险者,保户
19. a sum of money　一笔款项
20. value policy　定值保险单

Knowledge Consolidation 知识点巩固

在张先生的指导下,李娜掌握了有关货物保险的基本知识并阅读了一些有关保险的商务信函。但要确保书写一封好的商务信函,我们必须掌握以下关键词组和句型。我们一起来学学吧!

1. 表示投保、办理保险的固定搭配有:

cover insurance

arrange insurance

国际商务英语函电

effect insurance

provide insurance

take out insurance

2. 表示所保的货物，用介词 on。

e.g. insurance on the 100 tons of wool 对这 100 吨羊毛投保

表示投保的险别用介词 against。

e.g. insurance against All Risks 投保一切险

表示保额用介词 for。

e.g. insurance for 110% of the invoice value 按发票金额的 110%投保

表示保险费或保险费率用介词 at。

e.g. insurance at a slightly higher premium 以略高的保险费投保

表示向某保险公司投保用介词 with。

e.g. insurance with the People's Insurance Company of China 向中国人民保险公司投保

3. insurance amount　保险金额

insurance premium　保险费

insurance policy　保险单

insurance coverage　保险责任范围

insurance indemnity　保险赔偿

insurance rate　保险费率

special rate　特惠保率

4. make your rates available to us　让我方得知你方费率

5. for your account　由你方承担

6. ... forwarded to you　……被提交给你方

7. quote us a rate　报给我方(保险)费率

8. informing customer of insurance rate　通知客户保险费率

9. inform *sb*. of *sth*.　通知某人某事

10. the policy enclosed　随函附上保单一份

11. invoice value　发票金额,发票价值

12. Policy No.　保单号

13. claim payable at　赔款偿付地点

14. Invoice No. or B/L No.　发票号或提单号

15. per conveyance S.S.　运输工具

16. survey by　查勘代理人

17. amount insured　保险金额

18. Goods are normally insured for full amount of their value　货物通常全额保险

19. avoid all the possible risks, losses and damages　避免所有可能发生的风险、损失和损害

20. place orders on CIF basis　以到岸价格下订单

21. various kinds of risks　各式各样的风险

国际商务英语函电

22. the People's Insurance Company of China　中国人民保险公司

23. such as　诸如

24. cover a certain period of time　涵盖一定的时间段

25. be known as　被认为是

26. the former ... the latter　前者……后者

27. a small document issued by the insurance agents to their customers　一种由保险代理人向他们的客户开出的较小的文件

28. If you have any questions，just contact me.　如有问题就联系我。

29. The consignment is to be loaded on...　这批货将要装在……上。

30. sail from Shanghai on December 16 and is due in Pusan on December 19　于 12 月 16 日从上海起航预计于 12 月 19 日到达釜山

31. details with regard to...　关于……的细节

32. We would be grateful if you could quote a rate covering All Risks from port to port.　如果你方提出港对港一切险的报价，我方将不胜感激。

33. As the matter is urgent，we would appreciate a prompt reply.　由于事情紧急，如能迅速回复，我方将不胜感激。

34. We will issue a cover note as soon as you complete and return the enclosed declaration form.　一旦你方完成并寄回所附申报单，我方就会开出暂保单。

35. the net amount of the invoice　发票净值

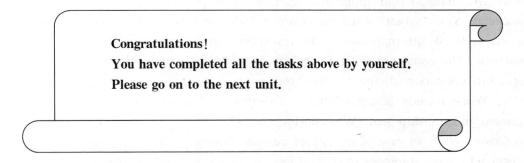

Congratulations！
You have completed all the tasks above by yourself.
Please go on to the next unit.

国际商务英语函电

Unit 11　Shipment

Situational Introduction 情景介绍

李娜勤奋好学,边实习、边学习国际商务知识。近来她在工作中接触到了有关装运方面的英语商务信函,虽然借助于一些工具书能够大致读懂,但是仍有很多困惑,很想全面了解有关装运方面的知识及专业术语。

装运是买卖双方执行合同的重要阶段,这一业务环节的函电主要围绕着租船订舱、报关发运以及单据制作等业务。张先生今天上午给李娜讲述了有关国际商务装运方面的知识,并向她展示了几封装运方面的商务信函。

BILLOF LADING
CHARTER PARTY
TRANSHIPMENT

Knowledge to Impart 知识传授

Li Na：Mr. Zhang, I find shipment is really a very important stage in international trade.

Mr. Zhang：Yes. In fact, shipment covers a wide range of work. Usually, three parties are involved in international trade transport：the consignor, the carrier and the consignee. The consignor delivers the goods to the consignee by the carrier. In some cases, brokers may participate in the process.

Li Na：When I study business letters on shipment, I meet some terms such as partial shipment and transhipment. What do they mean?

Mr. Zhang：Well, in case of an export business covering a large amount of goods, it is necessary to make shipment in several lots by several carriers sailing on different dates. This is partial shipment. When there are no ships sailing directly to the port of destination at the time, or the amount of cargo for a certain port of destination is so small that no ships would like to call at the port, transhipment is necessary. Of course, partial shipment and transhipment should be allowed by the buyers in advance.

Li Na：Can you tell me something about bill of lading?

Mr. Zhang：Yes. As soon as goods are loaded on board a ship, the shipping company should issue a bill of lading to the shipper, in other words, a bill of lading is a receipt of the goods. It states the conditions in which the goods were received by the shipper. The bill of lading, together with the insurance policy and the commercial invoice, constitute the chief shipping documents.

Li Na：Who designates the port of loading and the port of destination?

Mr. Zhang：In foreign trade, it is the seller who designates the port of loading or the

国际商务英语函电

convenience of shipping the goods, while the port of destination is usually designated by the buyer.

Li Na: I see, thank you. I've heard that sea transport is the most widely-used, is it?

Mr. Zhang: Well, there are five modes of transport: by sea, by road, by railway, by air, and by combined transport. Transport by sea is the most important mode of transportation in international trade, during which chartering of ships or booking shipping space is involved. The contract between the shipowner and the shipper may take the form of either a Charter Party or a bill of lading.

Li Na: Mr. Zhang, can you tell me the procedures for shipment of goods?

Mr. Zhang: The procedures for shipment of goods are rather complex. Before shipment, the exporter must:

- Find out freight rates;
- Select a shipment line and a particular vessel;
- Book shipping space;
- Register cargo on a shipping note and send it to a shipping company;
- Fill in the customs forms and send them to the Customs;
- Arrange adequate packing, including shipping marks;
- Obtain calling forward notice from the shipping company;
- Send goods to port with consignment note;
- Obtain bill of lading from the shipping company;
- Pay freight bill;
- Send the bill of lading to customer, or to the bank acting as intermediary.

Li Na: It is really a wide range of work. Do the exporters deal with all these by themselves?

Mr. Zhang: To save time and trouble, most exporters are inclined to use the services of shipping or forwarding agents who know all the different modes of transport best. The services include collecting the consignment and arranging shipment, and if packing and handling all documentation is required, also include making out the bill of lading, obtaining insurance, sending commercial invoices and paying the shipping company for their clients. The agents also inform the importer's forwarding agents that the shipment is on its way by sending an advice note, and they, in turn, will inform their client, send the goods on to him or her, or arrange for the goods to be stored until the goods are cleared through the Customs.

Li Na: Thank you, Mr. Zhang. I have taken you so much time.

Mr. Zhang: It doesn't matter. I think you are a hardworking girl. I'm always ready to give you some help. Now I'd like you to read the following example letters.

Li Na: OK, I'm so glad.

国际商务英语函电

China Transworld Shipping Corporation
3333 Beihai Street
Dalian

Ladies/Gentlemen，

We write to ask if you could find a ship of seven to eight thousand tons which we could charter for three months to ship soybeans from Dalian to various ports along the Japanese coast.

We will need a ship that is capable of making a fast turn round and will be able to manage at least ten trips within the period.

Very truly yours，
Jason Goodman
Senior Shipping Clerk
Nothgranary Cereals，Inc.
616 Taiyangdao Street
Harbin

Example Letter 2

Mr. Jason Goodman
Senior Shipping Clerk
Nothgranary Cereals，Inc.
616 Taiyangdao Street
Harbin

Dear Mr. Goodman，

Thank you for your fax of September 11. We are pleased to inform you that we have been able to secure the vessel you asked for.

She is the S. S. Bohai and is docked at present in Lianyungang. She has a cargo capacity of eight thousand tons. She is a bulk carrier，and has a speed of 24 knots，which will certainly enable her to make the number of trips you mentioned.

Please fax us to confirm the charter and we will send you the Charter Party.

Yours sincerely，
Li Lin
Charter Department
China Transworld Shipping Corporation
3333 Beihai Street
Dalian

Example Letter 3

Dear Sir or Madam，

As required in your letter of March 5th, we are pleased to provide the following information for your reference：

1. There are about 2 to 3 sailings weekly from Shanghai to Hong Kong.

2. Arrangements have been made with the ABC Line，which has one sailing approximately on the 10th every month from Hong Kong to West African ports，such as Lagos，Accra，etc. Shipping space is to be booked through their Shanghai agents，who communicate with the line by fax. After receipt of the Line's reply accepting the booking，their Shanghai agents will issue a Through Bill of Lading. Therefore，with the exception of unusual condition which may happen accidentally，the goods will be transhipped from Hong Kong without delay.

3. In general，the freight of transhipment from Hong Kong is higher than that from the U. K. or continental ports，but ABC Line agrees to the same freight，the detailed rates of which are shown on the two appendixes to this letter.

If you want to have the goods transhipped at Hong Kong，your letter of credit must reach us well before the shipment month so as to enable us to book space with the line's agents.

We assure you of our best attention at all times.

Yours faithfully，
Li Lin

Li Na has learned a lot from reading these example letters. Now Mr. Zhang is asking her to do more practice. It's also a good chance for us to learn. Let's do the practice together.

（从信函样张中，李娜学到了很多知识。现在张先生请她完成更多的练习，我们一起来参与吧）

 Practice 小·练习

Task 1：Answer the following questions.

1. What are the five main methods of transporting goods?

   _____

2. What is the most widely-used mode of transport in international trade?

   _____

3. Are the procedures for shipment of goods simple or complex?

   _____

4. Usually，how many parties are involved in international trade transport? What are they?

   _____

5. Do brokers participate in the process of transporting in some cases?

   _____

6. What are most exporters inclined to use in order to save time and trouble?

   _____

7. Can partial shipment and transhipment be allowed at any time?

   _____

8. Who designates the port of loading and the port of destination in foreign trade?

   _____

9. Can the bill of lading be sent to the bank acting as intermediary?

   _____

10. Does shipment cover a wide range of work?

    _____

Task 2：Decide whether the following statements are true or false.

(   ) 1. The first step of shipment is finding out freight rates.

(   ) 2. The consignee delivers the goods to the consignor by the carrier.

(   ) 3. Forwarding agents know all the different modes of transport best.

(   ) 4. Transport by rail is the most important mode of transport in international trade.

(   ) 5. The services of the forwarding agents include collecting the consignment and arranging shipment，and if packing and handling all documentation is required，also include making out the bill of lading，obtaining insurance，sending commercial invoices and paying the shipping company for their clients.

国际商务英语函电

Task 3: Choose the right answer for each sentence.

(   ) 1. As soon as goods are loaded on board a ship, _____ should issue a bill of lading.

    A. the buyer   B. the seller

    C. the shipping company   D. the bank

(   ) 2. We believe that you will have no difficulty _____ the goods in three lots.

    A. ship   B. shipping   C. shipped   D. to ship

(   ) 3. According to the contract stipulation, shipping marks are _____ the buyer's option.

    A. on   B. in   C. at   D. for

(   ) 4. To save time and trouble, most exporters _____ use the services of shipping or forwarding agents who know all the different modes of transport best.

    A. are inclined to   B. inclined to

    C. are inclining to   D. declined to

(   ) 5. We write to ask if you could find a ship of seven to eight thousand tons which we could _____ for three months to take shipments of soybeans from Dalian to various ports along the Japanese coast.

    A. charge   B. change   C. sail   D. charter

(   ) 6. We will need a ship that _____ making a fast turn round and will be able to manage at least ten trips within the period.

    A. is capable of   B. is able to   C. is capable to   D. is able of

(   ) 7. Thank you for your fax of September 11. We are pleased to inform you that we have been able to _____ the vessel you asked for.

    A. protect   B. secure   C. sail   D. drive

(   ) 8. S.S. Star has a cargo _____ of eight thousand tons.

    A. capacity   B. ability   C. length   D. size

(   ) 9. Shipping space _____ through their Shanghai agents, who communicate with the line by fax.

    A. is to book   B. is to be booking

    C. to be booked   D. is to be booked

(   ) 10. If you want to _____ at Hong Kong, your letter of credit must reach us well before the shipment month so as to enable us to book space with the line's agents.

    A. have the goods tranship

    B. have the goods transhipped

    C. had the goods transhipped

    D. have the goods transhipping

Task 4: Translation work.

A. Please put the following into Chinese.

1. Please fax us to confirm the charter and we will send you the Charter Party.

2. Their Shanghai agents will issue a Through Bill of Lading.

3. This vessel has a cargo capacity of eight thousand tons.

4. We are pleased to inform you that we have been able to secure the vessel you asked for.

B. Please put the following into English.

1. 发货人通过承运人把货物运交收货人。

2. 因这批货经香港转运，我们要求联运提单。

3. 海运在国际贸易中是最重要的运输模式。

4. 从上海到香港的运费由你方承担。

5. 由于没有直达船只，我们只好安排海陆联运。

Comments & Suggestions 评价及建议

李娜出色地完成了四项任务，现在要求她熟练掌握以下单词与词组。

1. shipment ['ʃɪpmənt] *n*. 装船，运货
2. stage [steɪdʒ] *n*. 阶段，进程
3. consignor [kən'saɪnə] *n*. 委托人，发货人
4. involve [ɪn'vɒlv] *v*. 牵涉，涉及
5. consignee [ˌkɒnsaɪ'niː] *n*. 收货人，收件人
6. carrier ['kærɪə] *n*. 承运人
7. participate [pɑː'tɪsɪpeɪt] *v*. 参与，参加

8. receipt [rɪ'siːt] *n*. 收据，收条
9. designate ['dezɪgneɪt] *v*. 指定
10. constitute ['kɒnstɪtjuːt] *v*. 组成
11. convenience [kən'viːnjəns] *n*. 便利，方便
12. mode [məʊd] *n*. 模式，方式
13. combine [kəm'baɪn] *v*. 使联合
14. charter ['tʃɑːtə] *v*. 租，包
15. procedure [prə'siːdʒə] *n*. 程序，手续

16. complex ['kɒmpleks] *a*. 复杂的

17. freight [freɪt] *n*. 运费，船

18. select [sɪ'lekt] *v*. 选择，挑选

19. vessel ['vesl] *n*. 船，舰

20. register ['redʒɪstə] *v*. 登记，记录

21. customs ['kʌstəmz] *n*. 海关

22. adequate ['ædɪkwɪt] *n*. 适当的，

足够的

23. obtain [əb'teɪn] *v*. 获得，得到

24. intermediary [ˌɪntə'miːdɪərɪ] *n*. 调解者，中间物

25. incline [ɪn'klaɪn] *v*. 使倾向于，使倾斜

● ●

1. cover a wide range of work 包括大范围的工作

2. in some cases 在某些情况下

3. in case of 假设，万一

4. a large amount of goods 大批量货物

5. in several lots 分几批

6. sailing on different dates 于不同日期起航

7. call at 停靠

8. be allowed by 被……允许

9. in advance 提前，预先

10. be loaded on board a ship 被装在船上

11. in other words 换句话说

12. commercial invoice 商业发票

13. port of loading 装货港

14. port of destination 目的港

15. combined transport 联合运输

16. book shipping space 订舱位

17. take the form of either a Charter Party or a bill of lading 采用租船契约或提单的形式

18. find out freight rates 查明运费

19. shipping note 装运通知单

20. fill in the customs forms 填写海关单据

21. arrange adequate packing 安排合适的包装

22. advice note 通知单，通知书

23. consignment note 托运通知

24. forwarding agent 货代公司，运输行

25. the bank acting as intermediary 作为中间人的银行

26. be inclined to ... 倾向于……

27. （the goods）be cleared through the Customs （货物）得以清关

Knowledge Consolidation 知识点巩固

在张先生的指导下，李娜掌握了有关货物装运的基本知识并做了大量的操练。为了巩固所学的知识要点，李娜必须掌握以下关键词组和句型。我们也一起来学学吧！

I. Useful phrases.

1. consignment 交付货物

2. consignment sale 意为"寄售"，对外贸易中的寄售是指出口人把货物运交在进口国的代理人或当地专营寄售业务的经纪人，委托后者代为销售。出口人又称为货主或委托人（consignor），受委托者又称为代售人或受货人（consignee）。寄售是有风险的出口方式，因为货物能否在进口市场销售，价格高低如何，事前都难以断定。

3. shipping documents 也称为 export documents，是货运单据、出口单据。在对外贸易业务中，出口汇票所附的海运提单（bill of lading）、保险单（insurance policy）及商业发票（commercial invoice）合称为货运单据。其他出口单据如领事签证单、化验证书、原产地证书、检验证明书及仓单等也随附汇票发出。

4. European Main Ports 常缩写为 EMP，指欧洲主要港口，如：意大利的热那亚（Genoa）、法国的马赛（Marseilles）、比利时的安特卫普（Antwerp）、荷兰的鹿特丹（Rotterdam）、英国的伦敦（London）、德国的汉堡（Hamburg）、丹麦的哥本哈根（Copenhagen）等。

5. shipping advice　装运通知

shipping agent　装运代理人

shipping company　船公司

shipping marks　运输唛头

shipping order　装运单

shipping space　舱位

6. through bill of lading　联运提单

7. with the exception of　除……之外

8. due　（车、船）预定应到的，预期的，约定的

9. shipping container　船运集装箱

10. S.S. Bohai　渤海轮（S.S. 是 steamship 的缩写）

11. urge / expedite shipment　加速发货，紧急发货

12. ETA（estimated time of arrival）　预计到达时间

ETD（estimated time of departure）　预计离开时间

13. non-negotiable bill of lading　不可转让提单

14. for one's reference　供某人参考

15. in advance　提前

16. timely delivery　准时发货

II. Useful sentences.

1. To save time and trouble，most exporters are inclined to use the services of shipping or forwarding agents who know all the different modes of transport best. 为了节省时间和减少麻烦，绝大多数出口商倾向于采用对各种运输模式最为了解的海运公司或货代公司的服务。

2. As the consignment is to be transhipped to Hong Kong，we require through B/L. 因这批货经香港转运，我们要求联运提单。

3. Please inform us of the name of the carrying vessel，the departure and the arrival time. 请告知货船的名字，以及出发和到达的时间。

4. Freight for shipment from Shanghai to Hong Kong is to be charged to your account. 从上海到香港的运费由你方承担。

5. The goods have been packed and marked exactly as directed so that they may be shipped by the first ship available towards the end of this month. 货物已严格按照要求包

装妥当并刷好唛头，这样就可由第一艘可用的船只于本月底运出。

6. Since there is no direct vessel，we have to arrange combined transport by rail and sea. 由于没有直达船只，我们只好安排海陆联运。

7. Would you please obtain for us a ship with a cargo capacity of about 4,000 tons? 请为我方找一条承载量约为四千吨的船只好吗？

8. We shall be glad to know the time of transit and the frequency of sailing，and whether cargo space should be reserved；if so，please send us the necessary application forms. 请告知运输途中的时间是多少，航次有多少，货船是否要预订；如需预订，请将订舱表寄来。

9. For the goods under our Contract No. SC456 we have booked space on S. S. 'East Wind' due to arrive in London around 19th May. 我们已在"东风轮"订妥舱位，以便装运合同号为 SC456 的货物，该轮约在五月十九日前后抵达伦敦。

10. Something unexpected compels us to seek cooperation by advancing your shipment of the goods under S/C No. 730 from August to July. 一些事先没有预料到的事情迫使我方寻求你方配合，请将 730 号销售确认书项下货物装运期由八月份提前到七月份。

Congratulations！
You have completed all the tasks above by yourself.
Please go on to the next unit.

Unit 12　Claims & Settlement

Situational Introduction 情景介绍

李娜实习的公司最近接到了一些客户的投诉函电，她阅读了其中一些信，从中知晓了投诉和处理投诉、索赔和理赔也是公司业务中司空见惯的事。她就这方面的问题和困惑来请教张先生。张先生给她讲解了投诉是如何发生的，发生之后该如何正确对待和妥善处理等等，要求她熟练地掌握常见的术语，以便更好地理解这方面的英语函电。

Knowledge to Impart 知识传授

Li Na：Mr. Zhang, we have received some complaining letters recently. Why does this happen?

Mr. Zhang：Well, you know, mistakes are inevitable. Ideally, it should not be necessary to complain, since in business everything should be done so carefully, details of offers and orders checked, packing supervised, quality control carried out expertly. Thus, there will be no mistakes made and nothing is damaged.

Li Na：If things are like what you said, it would be really ideal.

Mr. Zhang：Yes. But, unfortunately, as in other walks of life, things do not work out as well as that. Errors occur and goods are mishandled; accidents happen, usually because of haste and lack of supervision. There is often a shortage of staff owing to illness or holidays, and there is sometimes a shortage of sufficiently-trained staff.

Li Na：Are complaints similar?

Mr. Zhang：Complaints may be of several kinds and may arise from the delivery of wrong goods, damaged goods, or too many or too few goods. Even if the right articles are delivered in right quantities, they may arrive later than expected, thus causing severe difficulty to the buyer and, possibly, to his customers. Then the quality of the goods may be unsatisfactory; perhaps they may simply be second-rate products.

Li Na：What will happen if a customer is not satisfied?

Mr. Zhang：If a customer is dissatisfied with the execution of his order, he will complain. In doing so he should refer clearly to the articles in question, by referring to his order number or that of his supplier's invoice, or both. He should then specify the nature of his complaint, and finally state what action he wants his supplier to take.

Li Na: Mr. Zhang, How should we face all the complaints?

Mr. Zhang: Replies to complaints should always be courteous, even if the sellers think that the complaint is unfounded, they should not say it until they have good and reliable grounds to repudiate the claim. All complaints should be treated as serious matters and thoroughly investigated.

Li Na: Can you tell me the steps of dealing with complaints?

Mr. Zhang: On receiving the complaint, the sellers will make investigations, and if the complaint is justified, they will at once apologize to the buyers and suggest a solution. If the buyers have offered to keep the goods, the sellers will probably agree to them and give them a price reduction.

Li Na: Who determines the amount of the reduction?

Mr. Zhang: The amount of the reduction will depend on how bad the mistake is, and in some cases a substantial reduction, even with consequent loss, is of more advantage to the sellers than the expense and trouble of having the goods returned to them and causing inconvenience to their customers.

If the value of the goods in question is high, it may be advisable to have them returned, although the added risk of damage in further transport may not be worth incurring.

Li Na: Should the sellers make explanations to the buyers if they complain?

Mr. Zhang: There is no need for the sellers to go into a long story of how the mistake was made. A short explanation may be useful. But, generally speaking, the buyers are not interested in hearing how or why the error occurred but only in having the matter put right, in receiving the goods they ordered or at least the value for the money they have paid, or in knowing when they may expect to receive the delayed consignment.

Li Na: If the sellers are the first to find that a mistake has been made, what should they do?

Mr. Zhang: In that case, they should not wait for complaining, but should write, telex or fax at once to let the buyers know, and either put the matter right or offer some compensation.

Li Na: Thank you very much, Mr. Zhang, but I need to read more letters on complaints and settlement.

Mr. Zhang: OK. I will gather some for you.

Example Letter 1

Mr. Rob Subbarama
Export Manager
Nusantara Trading Co. Ltd.
Alan Malaks No. 51
Jakarta, Indonesia

国际商务英语函电

Dear Mr. Rob Subbarama,

We have received the documents and taken delivery of the above order which arrived at Kowloon on the M. V. Toho Maru.

On checking the goods we found that Carton No. 13 contained only 15,000 Coconut Ball Pens, although 24,000 had been entered on both the packing list and the invoice.

The full consignment is urgently required to complete orders for three of our major customers so it is absolutely essential that you ship the additional 9,000 ball pens on the earliest possible flight from Jakarta.

This is the third time in the last twelve months that you have short-shipped one of our orders. If there is any further repetition of this, we will be forced to look for an alternative supplier.

Sincerely yours,
Li Lin
Deputy Manager

Example Letter 2

Li Na
Deputy Manager
New Times Trading Company Limited
13 – 14 / F Industry Building
Hong Kong, China

Dear Miss Li Lin,

Thank you for your fax of 17 January. We are extremely sorry to learn that an error was made in Carton No. 13 of the above order.

国际商务英语函电

The missing 9,000 ball pens were sent this morning by Cathay Airways and the documents have already been forwarded to you.

We greatly regret the inconvenience caused by this and the previous two errors, and offer our sincere apologies. We can assure you that every effort will be made to ensure that similar errors do not occur again.

Yours sincerely,
Rob Subbarama
Export Manager

Example Letter 3

China National & Export Corp.
Shanghai
China

Dear Sir or Madam,

We are sorry to hear that you have had trouble with your "716 machine".

We have asked our service department to have a thorough investigation of the matter, and they report that the difficulty in starting was due to your using a heavy motor oil in the tank instead of the light grade that we specifically recommend in the handbook.

The reason for the final stoppage was a seized bearing caused by the fact that it had not been greased. Though our guarantee covers faulty material and workmanship, it does not, as you will realize, cover damage done by improper use or negligence of maintenance. The bearings on all our machines are thoroughly greased before they leave our workshop, and you are advised in the handbook that greasing is necessary at regular intervals.

In these circumstances, we think you will agree that we can't be expected to grant a free replacement of these damaged parts. However, we are willing to compromise by replacing them at the bare cost of new materials alone. The charge for that will be £ 135. New bearings will be put in and the machine will be thoroughly cleaned and greased.

国际商务英语函电

If you drop us a line authorizing us to do this, we will send our technicians to proceed with the work at once, and you will have the machine in first rate working condition.

We hope you will feel that this concession on our part is a satisfactory solution to the difficulty.

Yours truly,
Universal Industry Co. Ltd.

Li Na is very excellent as a trainee. She catches every minute to study hard. Look, she is doing some practice again!

（作为一名实习生，李娜是非常优秀的，她总是抓住机会努力学习。瞧，她又进行操练啦）

 Practice·小练习

Task 1: Answer the following questions.

1. Why do some customers complain?

2. What may complaints arise from?

3. When should the sellers make investigations?

4. Are the buyers interested in hearing how or why the error occurred?

5. Should all complaints be treated as serious matters and thoroughly investigated?

6. If the complaint is justified, what should the sellers do first?

7. Should replies to complaints be courteous?

8. If the value of the goods in question is high, what will the sellers possibly do?

9. If the buyers have offered to keep the goods, what will the amount of price reduction depend on?

10. If the sellers are the first to find that a mistake has been made, what should they do?

_____

Task 2: Decide whether the following statements are true or false.

(   ) 1. Errors occur, goods are mishandled and accidents happen, usually because of haste and lack of supervision.

(   ) 2. It is necessary for the sellers to go into a long story of how the mistake was made.

(   ) 3. If a customer is dissatisfied with the execution of his order, he will complain.

(   ) 4. Even if the right articles are delivered in the right quantities, they may arrive later than expected, thus causing severe difficulty to the buyer and, possibly, to his customers.

(   ) 5. In case the sellers are the first to discover that a mistake has been made, they should wait for a complaint.

Task 3: Choose the right answer for each sentence.

(   ) 1. _____ the buyers are not interested in hearing how or why the error occurred but only in having the matter put right.
   A. Generally speaking   B. General speaking
   C. Generally speak   D. General speak

(   ) 2. _____ checking the goods we found that Carton No. 13 contained only 15,000 Coconut Ball Pens, although 24,000 had been entered on both the packing list and the invoice.
   A. In   B. At   C. On   D. From

(   ) 3. This is the third time in the last twelve months that you _____ one of our orders.
   A. have short-ship   B. had short-ship
   C. have short-shipped   D. have been short-shipped

(   ) 4. If there is any _____ repetition of this we will be forced to look for an alternative supplier.
   A. further   B. farther   C. far   D. fur

(   ) 5. The missing 9,000 ball pens were sent this morning by Cathay Airways and the documents have already been _____ to you.
   A. taken   B. brought   C. carried   D. forwarded

(   ) 6. Replies to complaints should always be _____.
   A. courteous   B. rough   C. impolite   D. disputed

(　　) 7. The amount of price reduction will depend on _____.
　　　　A. how bad the weather is　　　　B. how good the friendship is
　　　　C. how bad the health is　　　　D. how bad the mistake is

(　　) 8. If the value of the goods in question is _____, it may be advisable
　　　　to have them returned.
　　　　A. low　　　　　B. high　　　　　C. a little　　　　D. less

(　　) 9. If the buyers have offered to keep the goods, the sellers will probably
　　　　_____ a price reduction.
　　　　A. agree with　　B. agree to　　　C. disagree with　D. disagree to

(　　) 10. _____, it should not be necessary to complain, since in business
　　　　everything should be done so carefully, details of offers and orders
　　　　checked, packing supervised, quality control carried out expertly.
　　　　A. Unfortunately　　　　　　　B. Fortunately
　　　　C. Expertly　　　　　　　　　D. Ideally

Task 4: Translation Work.

A. Please put the following into Chinese.

1. This is the third time in the last twelve months that you. . . _____

2. be forced to look for an alternative supplier _____

3. be extremely sorry to learn that. . . _____

4. the inconvenience caused by this _____

5. to ensure that similar errors do not occur again _____

B. Please put the following into English.

1. 向顾客道歉 _____

2. 缺乏员工 _____

3. 一接到投诉就…… _____

4. 给予某种补偿 _____

5. 接踵而来的损失 _____

 Comments & Suggestions 评价及建议

李娜出色地完成了四项任务,现在要求她熟练掌握以下单词和词组。

1. complaint [kəm'pleɪnt] n. 抱怨,
投诉

2. inevitable [ɪn'evɪtəbl] a. 不可避免
的

3. ideal [aɪ'dɪəl] a. 理想的

4. supervise ['sjuːpəvaɪz] v. 监督

5. unfortunately [ʌn'fɔːtʃənɪtlɪ] adv.
不幸地,遗憾地

6. error ['erə] *n*. 出错

7. occur [ə'kɜ:] *v*. 发生，出现

8. mishandle [mɪs'hændl] *n*. 错误地处理，胡乱操作

9. haste [heɪst] *n*. 匆忙，急忙

10. sufficiently [sə'fɪʃəntlɪ] *adv*. 充分地

11. unsatisfactory [ˌʌnsætɪs'fæktərɪ] *a*. 令人不满意的

12. second-rate ['sekənd'reɪt] *a*. 二流的

13. execution [ˌeksɪ'kjuːʃən] *n*. 执行

14. specify ['spesɪfaɪ] *v*. 指定，详细说明

15. face [feɪs] *v*. 面对

16. courteous ['kɜːtɪəs] *a*. 有礼貌的

17. unfounded [ʌn'faʊndɪd] *a*. 没有理由的

18. repudiate [rɪ'pjuːdɪeɪt] *v*. 批判，驳倒

19. reliable [rɪ'laɪəbl] *a*. 可靠的

20. thoroughly ['θʌrəlɪ] *adv*. 彻底地

21. investigate [ɪn'vestɪgeɪt] *v*. 调查

22. solution [sə'luːʃən] *n*. 解决办法

23. reduction [rɪ'dʌkʃən] *n*. 减少，降低

24. determine [dɪ'tɜːmɪn] *v*. 决定

25. substantial [səb'stænʃəl] *a*. 实质的

26. consequent ['kɒnsɪˌkwent] *a*. 随之发生的

27. advantage [əd'vɑːntɪdʒ] *n*. 优势

28. advisable [əd'vaɪzəbl] *a*. 明智的

29. incur [ɪn'kɜː] *v*. 招致

30. compensation [ˌkɒmpən'seɪʃən] *n*. 补偿，赔偿

31. stoppage ['stɒpɪdʒ] *n*. 停止，填塞

32. concession [kən'seʃən] *n*. 让步

• •

1. complaining letter 投诉信

2. quality control 质量控制，质量管理

3. carry out 完成，实现，贯彻，执行

4. walk of life 行业，职业

5. work out 解决，算出

6. be mishandled 胡乱操作

7. as well as 也，又

8. lack of supervision 缺乏监督

9. a shortage of staff 缺乏员工

10. trained staff 训练有素的员工

11. arise from ... 起于……

12. in right quantity 数量正确

13. second-rate product 二等产品

14. be dissatisfied with ... 对……不满

15. refer clearly to ... 清楚地指明……

16. the articles in question 上述产品

17. take action 采取行动

18. reply to complaint 回复投诉信

19. thoroughly investigate 彻底调查

20. suggest a solution 提出解决方案

21. agree to a price reduction 同意降价

22. the amount of the reduction 降价额

23. consequent loss 随之造成的损失

24. have the goods returned to ... 把货物返还给……

25. the added risk 增加风险

26. there is no need for *sb*. to do ... 对某人来说没必要做……

27. go into a long story 长篇大论

28. generally speaking 一般而言

29. have the matter put right 把事情做对

Knowledge Consolidation 知识点巩固

在张先生的指导下,李娜掌握了有关投诉和处理投诉、索赔和理赔的贸易知识。但要确保书写一封好的商务信函,我们和李娜一样必须掌握以下关键词组和句型。我们一起来学学吧!

I. Useful phrases.

1. claim   索赔,要求赔偿

后接介词 for,表示索赔的原因,如:claim for a damage;

后接介词 for 也可表示索赔的金额,如:claim for USD 10,000;

后接介词 on,表示对某批货物索赔,如:claim on the goods;

后接介词 against,表示向某人索赔,如:claim against the underwriters。

2. claim for inferior quality   对质量低劣提出索赔

3. lodge claims against / with *sb*.   向某人提出索赔

4. look into the matter   调查该事件

5. SOP（Standard Operation Procedure）标准作业书

6. cover your loss   弥补贵方的损失

7. sufficient replacement   充足的替代物

8. considerably overdue   严重延误

9. on the understanding that ...   在知悉……的情况下

II. Useful sentences.

1. You should be entirely responsible for the loss we sustained owing to improper packing. 因不良包装使我方承受的损失,你方应全权负责。

2. We have to sell your electric fans at greatly reduced price. 我们不得不大幅降价来出售你方的电风扇。

3. After re-inspection, we found that the quality of your goods was not in conformity with the contracted stipulations. 复验之后,我方发现产品质量与合同规定不符。

4. The buyer has filed a claim on the shipment for USD 500.00. 买方已对货物提出了索赔 500 美元的要求。

5. We trust that this arrangement will satisfy you and make up your total loss. 我方相信这样的安排会令您感到满意,并且弥补你方所有的损失。

6. We deeply apologize for our mistakes and promise you we will correct it at once. 针对我方的错误,我方向您表示深深的歉意,并承诺马上纠正这一错误。

7. We suggest you'd better lodge a claim against the shipping company since the damage is caused by careless handling while in transit. 鉴于该损坏是由于运输途中的随意处置引起的,我方建议你方最好向船公司提出申诉。

8. We are much obliged / appreciated to you for your help. 我们非常感激您对我们的帮助。

9. We will spare no efforts to support you so as to solve this problem. 我们将不遗余

力地帮您解决这一问题。

10. We have sent you USD 300.00 by T / T today in settlement of your claim for shortage of 100 pieces. 我方已电汇给你方 300 美元来支付你方有关短量 100 件的索赔。

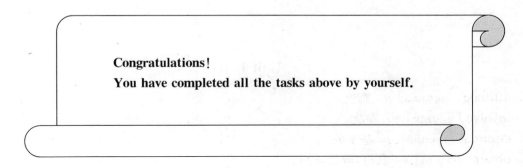

Congratulations!
You have completed all the tasks above by yourself.

国际商务英语函电

Appendix I　New Words and Phrases to Each Unit

Unit 1

1. attitude ['ætɪtjuːd] *n*. 态度
2. involve [ɪn'vɒlv] *v*. 涉及
3. essential [ɪ'senʃəl] *a*. 基本的
4. obtain [əb'teɪn] *v*. 获得，取得，得到
5. tactful ['tæktfəl] *a*. 得体的，圆滑的
6. clearness ['klɪənɪs] *n*. 清楚
7. conciseness [kən'saɪsnɪs] *n*. 简洁
8. consideration [kən,sɪdə'reɪʃən] *n*. 周到
9. courtesy ['kɜːtəsɪ] *n*. 礼貌
10. concreteness ['kɒnkriːtnɪs] *n*. 具体
11. correctness [kə'rektnɪs] *n*. 正确
12. completeness [kəm'pliːtnɪs] *n*. 完整
13. principle ['prɪnsəpl] *n*. 原则
14. positive ['pɒzɪtɪv] *a*. 主动的
15. conversational [,kɒnvə'seɪʃənl] *a*. 对话的
16. personable ['pɜːsənəbl] *a*. 优雅的，风度翩翩的，貌美的
17. specification [,spesɪfɪ'keɪʃən] *n*. 规格
18. commission [kə'mɪʃən] *n*. 佣金，手续费
19. appreciative [ə'priːʃɪətɪv] *a*. 表示赞赏的，感谢的
20. prompt [prɒmpt] *a*. 敏捷的，及时的，迅速的

• •

1. straight-forward words　易懂的话
2. wordy statement　啰唆的写法
3. fancy language　花哨的用词
4. bear in mind　牢记在心
5. modest tone　谦虚的口吻
6. be prompt in reply　及时回复
7. vivid and exact words　生动准确的话
8. minor mistake　小错误
9. above-mentioned　以上所提到的
10. lose out　输掉，失败

国际商务英语函电

Unit 2

1. particular [pə'tɪkjʊlə] *n*. 详细情况
2. postcode ['pəʊstˌkəʊd] *n*. 邮政编码
3. letterhead ['letəˌhed] *n*. 信头
4. communication [kəˌmjuːnɪ'keɪʃən] *n*. 通信，交往
5. logo ['ləʊgəʊ] *n*. 公司标志
6. stationery ['steɪʃənərɪ] *n*. 信纸，文具
7. vital ['vaɪtl] *a*. 重要的
8. logical ['lɒdʒɪkəl] *a*. 合理的，逻辑的
9. cardinal ['kɑːdɪnl] *a*. 基本的
10. ordinal ['ɔːdɪnəl] *a*. 顺序的
11. confuse [kən'fjuːz] *v*. 混淆，搞乱
12. comma ['kɒmə] *n*. 逗号
13. salutation [ˌsæljʊ'teɪʃən] *n*. 称呼
14. acquaint [ə'kweɪnt] *v*. 使了解，使熟悉
15. summation [sʌ'meɪʃən] *n*. 概括
16. complimentary [ˌkɒmplɪ'mentərɪ] *a*. 表示敬意的
17. signature ['sɪgnɪtʃə] *n*. 签名
18. align [ə'laɪn] *v*. 排列，对齐
19. silk [sɪlk] *n*. 丝绸，丝织物

•••••••••••••••••••••••••••••••••

1. business communication　商务交流
2. principal part　主要部分
3. as follows　如下
4. standard form　标准形式
5. logical order　逻辑次序
6. cardinal number　基数
7. ordinal number　序数
8. ZIP code　邮政编码
9. be acquainted with ...　与……熟悉
10. positive response　肯定的答复
11. be in keeping with ...　与……保持一致
12. well-constructed　构思完美的
13. supplementary element　附加部分
14. full blocked format　完全齐头式
15. semi-blocked format　半齐头式或混合式
16. on the contrary　相反

国际商务英语函电

Unit 3

1. initial [ɪˈnɪʃəl] *a*. 开始的，初次的
2. status [ˈsteɪtəs] *n*. 情况，状况
3. prospective [prəˈspektɪv] *a*. 未来的
4. counselor [ˈkaʊnsələ] *n*. 顾问，参事
5. commercial [kəˈmɜːʃəl] *a*. 商业的，商务的
6. delegation [ˌdelɪˈgeɪʃən] *n*. 代表团
7. investigation [ɪnˌvestɪˈgeɪʃən] *n*. 调查，研究
8. financial [faɪˈnænʃəl] *a*. 财政的，金融的
9. reputation [ˌrepjʊˈteɪʃən] *n*. 名誉，名声
10. quotation [kwəʊˈteɪʃən] *n*. 报价，引用
11. appreciate [əˈpriːʃɪeɪt] *v*. 欣赏，感激
12. furnish [ˈfɜːnɪʃ] *v*. 供应，提供
13. substantial [səbˈstænʃəl] *a*. 大量的，丰盛的
14. embroider [ɪmˈbrɔɪdə] *v*. 绣（花纹）（+ on）
15. assorted [əˈsɔːtɪd] *a*. 各种各样，合适的
16. approach [əˈprəʊtʃ] *v*. 接近，与……联系
17. separately [ˈsepərɪtlɪ] *adv*. 各自地，分别地
18. forthwith [ˈfɔːθˈwɪð] *adv*. 立刻，马上
19. irrevocable [ɪˈrevəkəbl] *a*. 不可撤销的
20. potential [pəˈtenʃəl] *a*. 潜在的，可能的
21. guarantee [ˌgærənˈtiː] *n*. 保证书 *v*. 担保
22. corresponding [ˌkɒrɪˈspɒndɪŋ] *a*. 一致的
23. transaction [trænˈzækʃən] *n*. 交易，买卖
24. recommendation [ˌrekəmenˈdeɪʃən] *n*. 推荐
25. catalog [ˈkætəlɒg] *n*. 产品目录

••••••••••••••••••••••••••••••••••••••

1. prospective customer   潜在客户
2. first important step   首要的一步
3. Chambers of Commerce in foreign countries   国外商会
4. Commercial Counselor's Office   商务参赞处
5. trade fair   交易会
6. mutual visits   互访
7. establish business relations   建立贸易关系
8. status investigation   资信调查
9. financial position   财务状况
10. East-China Fair   华东交易会
11. specialize in   专门经营

12. be in the market for 要买(货物)

13. at *sb*.'s end 在某人处

14. upon receipt of *sth*. 一收到某物,就……

15. embroidered table-cloth 绣花台布

16. lowest quotation 最低报价

17. credit standing 信用状况

18. on a substantial scale 批量

19. assorted colors 各种各样的颜色

20. respective price list 各自的价目表

21. leading importers 主要进口商

Unit 4

1. inform [ɪnˈfɔːm] *v*. 通知

2. enlarge [ɪnˈlɑːdʒ] *v*. 扩大

3. addition [əˈdɪʃən] *n*. 增加

4. various [ˈveərɪəs] *a*. 各种各样的

5. sample [ˈsæmpl] *n*. 样品

6. quote [kwəʊt] *v*. 报价

7. assurance [əˈʃʊərəns] *n*. 保证

8. region [ˈriːdʒən] *n*. 地区

9. request [rɪˈkwest] *v*. & *n*. 要求

10. prompt [prɒmpt] *a*. 及时的

11. discount [ˈdɪskaʊnt] *n*. 折扣

12. advise [ədˈvaɪz] *v*. 告知

13. tip [tɪp] *n*. 建议

14. promote [prəˈməʊt] *v*. 促进

15. blouse [blaʊz] *n*. 女式衬衫

16. perusal [pəˈruːzl] *n*. 细读

17. utensil [juːˈtensl] *n*. 器具,用具;器皿;家庭厨房用具

18. range [reɪndʒ] *n*. 范围;射程;类别

19. draft [drɑːft] *n*. 汇票

20. enclosed [ɪnˈkləʊzd] *a*. 被附上的

21. negotiate [nɪˈgəʊʃɪeɪt] *v*. 谈判,协商,交涉

22. deliver [dɪˈlɪvə] *v*. 发表;递送;交付

23. settlement [ˈsetlmənt] *n*. 解决;结算

24. trust [trʌst] *n*. & *v*. 相信,信任

25. refer [rɪˈfɜː] *v*. 提到;针对;关系到;请教

26. intend [ɪnˈtend] *v*. 意欲,计划

27. commission [kəˈmɪʃən] *n*. 佣金,手续费

国际商务英语函电

28. delivery [dɪˈlɪvərɪ] n. 传送，投递；(正式)交付
29. occasion [əˈkeɪʒən] n. 机会，时机；场合
30. regard [rɪˈgɑːd] n. & v. 关系；注意
31. trade [treɪd] v. & n. 贸易；行业；买卖
32. hesitate [ˈhezɪteɪt] v. 犹豫，踌躇

• •

1. fit in   适合
2. supply from stock   现货供应
3. put ... into market   投放市场
4. right away   立即
5. of great importance   非常重要
6. attempt to   试图
7. have faith in   有信心
8. at sight   即期
9. chemical fertilizer   化工肥料

Unit 5

1. available [əˈveɪləbl] a. 可得的；空闲的
2. transaction [trænˈzækʃən] n. 交易；事务
3. relevant [ˈrelɪvənt] a. 有关的；中肯的
4. disagreement [dɪsəˈgriːmənt] n. 不一致；争论；意见不同
5. amendment [əˈmendmənt] n. 改正，修改
6. limitation [ˌlɪmɪˈteɪʃən] n. 限制；限度；有效期限
7. properly [ˈprɒpəlɪ] adv. 适当地；正确地；恰当地
8. essential [ɪˈsenʃəl] a. 基本的；必要的
9. element [ˈelɪmənt] n. 元素；要素
10. discount [ˈdɪskaʊnt] n. 折扣
11. payment [ˈpeɪmənt] n. 支付
12. indication [ˌɪndɪˈkeɪʃən] n. 指示，指出
13. packing [ˈpækɪŋ] n. 包装；填充物
14. carriage [ˈkærɪdʒ] n. 运输；运费
15. insurance [ɪnˈʃʊərəns] n. 保险；保险费
16. quotation [kwəʊˈteɪʃən] n. (贸易)报价单
17. considerate [kənˈsɪdərɪt] a. 体贴的；体谅的；考虑周到的
18. attitude [ˈætɪtjuːd] n. 态度
19. superior [suːˈpɪərɪə] a. 上级的；优秀的，出众的
20. item [ˈaɪtəm] n. 条款；项目；一件商品(或物品)
21. willingness [ˈwɪlɪŋnɪs] n. 自愿，乐意

22. period ['pɪərɪəd] *n*. 时期；(一段)时间

23. validity [və'lɪdɪtɪ] *n*. 有效，合法性

24. negotiable [nɪ'gəʊʃəbəl] *a*. 可谈判的；可协商的；(票据)可兑现的

25. alternative [ɔ:l'tɜ:nətɪv] *a*. 两者择一的

26. capability [ˌkeɪpə'bɪlɪtɪ] *n*. 才能，能力；生产率

27. competitor [kəm'petɪtə] *n*. 竞争者；对手

28. complicated ['kɒmplɪkeɪtɪd] *a*. 结构复杂的；混乱的，麻烦的

29. conform [kən'fɔ:m] *v*. 符合；遵照；适应环境

30. Vancouver [væn'ku:və] *n*. [地名](加拿大)温哥华

31. shipment ['ʃɪpmənt] *n*. 装运；载货量

32. margin ['mɑ:dʒɪn] *n*. 利润，盈余

33. justify ['dʒʌstɪfaɪ] *v*. 证明……有理；对……作出解释

34. one-shot ['wʌnʃɒt] *a*. 只有一次的

35. manufacturer [ˌmænjʊ'fæktʃərə] *n*. 制造商，制造厂；厂主

36. standard ['stændəd] *n*. 标准，规格　*a*. 标准的，合格的

37. trend [trend] *n*. 走向；趋向

38. dominate ['dɒmɪneɪt] *v*. 控制；在……中占首要地位

39. customize ['kʌstəˌmaɪz] *vt*. 定制，定做；按规格改制

40. blend [blend] *v*. 混合；把……掺在一起

• •

1. figure out　发现，明白

2. exchange rate　汇率

3. firm offer　实盘

4. final confirmation　最终确认

Unit 6

Part 1　Orders

1. inform [ɪn'fɔ:m] *v*. 通知，告知

2. sample ['sæmpl] *n*. 样例，样张

3. satisfactory [ˌsætɪs'fæktərɪ] *a*. 令人感到满意的

4. urgent ['ɜ:dʒənt] *a*. 急切的，迫切的

5. specification [ˌspesɪfɪ'keɪʃən] *n*. 规格，产品说明

6. quantity ['kwɒntɪtɪ] *n*. 数量

7. destination [ˌdestɪ'neɪʃən] *n*. 目的地

8. enclosed [ɪn'kləʊzd] *a*. 随信附上

9. pillow ['pɪləʊ] *n*. 枕头

10. primrose ['prɪmrəʊz] *a*. 淡黄色的

11. bale [beɪl] *n*. 大包

12. L/C (letter of credit) *n*. 信用证
13. commodity [kə'mɒdɪtɪ] *n*. 商品,货物

••

1. order No.　订单号
2. make delivery　发货
3. at an early date　早期
4. place an order　下订单
5. bed sheet　床单
6. pillow case　枕头套
7. cotton cloth bale　棉布大包
8. irrevocable L/C　不可撤销信用证
9. draft at sight　即期汇票
10. terms of payment　付款方式

Part 2　Contracts

1. mutually ['mju:tʃʊəlɪ] *adv*. 相互地
2. agreement [ə'gri:mənt] *n*. 协议
3. preamble [pri:'æmbl] *n*. 约首
4. shipment ['ʃɪpmənt] *n*. 装运
5. confirmation [ˌkɒnfə'meɪʃən] *n*. 确认
6. valid ['vælɪd] *a*. 有效的
7. herewith [hɪə'wɪð] *adv*. 同此
8. covering ['kʌvərɪŋ] *a*. 涉及……的
9. stipulation [ˌstɪpjʊ'leɪʃən] *n*. 规定
10. subsequent ['sʌbsɪkwənt] *a*. 后来的
11. inspection [ɪn'spekʃən] *n*. 检验
12. claim [kleɪm] *n*. 索赔
13. arbitration [ˌɑːbɪ'treɪʃn] *n*. 仲裁
14. seal [si:l] *n*. 盖章
15. undermentioned ['ʌndə'menʃənd] *a*. 下述的
16. illustrate ['ɪləstreɪt] *v*. 说明;表明;给……加插图
17. trial ['traɪəl] *n*. 试验　*a*. 试验的

••

1. order *sth*. from *sb*.　向某人订购某物
2. witness clauses　约尾
3. port of destination　到达港
4. force majeure　不可抗力
5. in duplicate　一式两份
6. for our file　以便我们存档

7. in one's favor/in favor of　对……有益
8. see to it that　一定做到
9. conform with　与……保持一致
10. may rest assured　请放心

Unit 7

1. covering ['kʌvərɪŋ] v. 关于
2. await [ə'weɪt] v. 等待
3. proposal [prə'pəʊzəl] n. 提议，建议
4. instruct [ɪn'strʌkt] v. 通知，指示
5. banker ['bæŋkə] n. 银行
6. substantial [səb'stænʃəl] a. 数量大的
7. initial [ɪ'nɪʃəl] a. 首次的
8. conclude [kən'kluːd] v. 达成，完成(交易)
9. execute ['eksɪkjuːt] v. 执行
10. gnawing ['nɔːɪŋ] a. 折磨人的，令人痛苦的
11. exception [ɪk'sepʃən] n. 例外
12. exceptional [ɪk'sepʃənl] a. 例外的
13. conducive [kən'djuːsɪv] a. 有助于……；有益于……
14. facilitate [fə'sɪlɪteɪt] v. 促进；帮助；使……容易
15. precedent ['presɪdənt] n. 先例
16. consignment [kən'saɪnmənt] n. 托运的货物
17. s. s. = steam ship [stiːmʃɪp] n. 轮船
18. draw [drɔː] v. 开出汇票
19. drawer ['drɔːə] n. 出票人，开汇票人
20. drawee [drɔː'iː] n. 受票人，付款人
21. reiterate [riː'ɪtəreɪt] v. 重申
22. earthenware ['ɜːθənˌweə] n. 陶器

1. in value　在价值上
2. on ... basis = on the basis of　以……为基础；按……条件
3. Cash Against Documents (C. A. D.)　付款交单
4. Cash with Order (C. W. O.)　随订单付现
5. Cash on Delivery (C. O. D.)　交货付现/付现交单
6. meet with　满足
7. the unpaid balance　未付的余款
8. tie up　冻结
9. liquid funds　流动资金

10. on or before   截止

11. with regard to   关于

12. prove to be   证明是……

13. in view of   鉴于

14. easier payment terms   宽松的付款方式

15. under present circumstances   在目前情况下

16. as far as ... be concerned   关于……

17. usual practice   通常惯例

18. make payment   付款

19. trial order   试订单

20. shipping documents   装船单据

21. Standard Chartered Bank   渣打银行

22. regret doing *sth*.   对做过的事感到遗憾

Unit 8

1. undertake [ˌʌndəˈteɪk] *v*. 承担,着手做;同意,答应

2. beneficiary [ˌbenɪˈfɪʃərɪ] *n*. 受益人,受惠者

3. reliable [rɪˈlaɪəbl] *a*. 可信赖的;可靠的;确实的

4. issue [ˈɪʃuː] *v*. 发行

5. exceed [ɪkˈsiːd] *v*. 超过;胜过

6. triplicate [ˈtrɪplɪkɪt] *a*. 一式三份的

7. duplicate [ˈdjuːplɪkɪt] *a*. 一式两份的

8. negotiable [nɪˈɡəʊʃəbl] *a*. 可协商的

9. honor [ˈɒnə] *v*. 承兑,支付;允准;实践

10. endorse [ɪnˈdɔːs] *v*. 在(发票、票据等)背面签名,背书

11. sufficient [səˈfɪʃənt] *a*. 足够的,充分的

12. dispatch [dɪˈspætʃ] *v*. 派遣;发送;快递

13. expedite [ˈekspɪdaɪt] *v*. 迅速执行;促进

14. discrepancy [dɪsˈkrepənsɪ] *n*. 不一致,不符,差异

15. amend [əˈmend] *v*. 修改

16. read [riːd] *v*. 读起来,写明

17. presentation [ˌprezənˈteɪʃən] *n*. 陈述;报告;介绍;赠送

18. hereby [hɪəˈbaɪ] *adv*. 以此方式,特此

19. establish [ɪˈstæblɪʃ] *v*. 建立,创建

20. exceed [ɪkˈsiːd] *v*. 超过;超越

21. partial [ˈpɑːʃəl] *a*. 部分的

• •

1. draw on(upon)   开立

2. certificate of origin　原产地证明书

3. with reference to　关于

4. up to　直到(现在)

5. do one's utmost　尽某人最大努力

6. in accordance with　与……一致

7. bill of lading　提单

8. due to　由于

9. by cable　用电报发出

10. freight prepaid　运费预付,运费已付

Unit 9

1. dress [dres] *v.* (给……)穿衣

2. especially [ɪ'speʃəlɪ] *adv.* 特别,尤其

3. art [ɑːt] *n.* 艺术

4. grasp [ɡrɑːsp] *v.* 掌握,领会,抓住

5. content ['kɒntent] *n.* 内容,容量

6. compact [kəm'pækt] *a.* 结实的

7. rough [rʌf] *a.* 粗糙的;崎岖不平的

8. shape [ʃeɪp] *n.* 外形,形状,形态

9. journey ['dʒɜːnɪ] *n.* 旅行,旅程

10. condition [kən'dɪʃən] *n.* 情况;状态

11. particular [pə'tɪkjʊlə] *a.* 值得注意的;特别的;不寻常的

12. destination [ˌdestɪ'neɪʃən] *n.* 目的地

13. load [ləʊd] *v.* 装载,装填,使担负

14. unload [ʌn'ləʊd] *v.* 卸货

15. reload [riː'ləʊd] *v.* 再装

16. department [dɪ'pɑːtmənt] *n.* 部,局,处

17. establish [ɪ'stæblɪʃ] *v.* 成立,建立

18. regular ['reɡjʊlə] *a.* 有规律的

19. review [rɪ'vjuː] *n.* 回顾;再检查

20. method ['meθəd] *n.* 方法;办法

21. ensure [ɪn'ʃʊə] *v.* 确保,保证

22. specialist ['speʃəlɪst] *n.* 专家,行家

23. infuriating [ɪn'fjʊərɪˌeɪtɪŋ] *a.* 令人发怒的

24. customer ['kʌstəmə] *n.* 消费者

25. secure [sɪ'kjʊə] *v.* 保护,使安全

26. freight [freɪt] *n.* 运费,货物,货运

27. convenience [kən'viːnjəns] *n.* 便利,方便

28. container [kən'teɪnə] *n.* 容器,集装箱

国际商务英语函电

29. vary ['veərɪ] *v*. 变化

30. carton ['kɑːtən] *n*. 硬纸盒

31. case [keɪs] *n*. 箱，盒

32. crate [kreɪt] *n*. 板条

33. drum [drʌm] *n*. 鼓型圆桶箱

34. barrel ['bærəl] *n*. 桶

35. carboy ['kɑːbɔɪ] *n*. 玻璃瓶，钢瓶

36. beforehand [bɪ'fɔːˌhænd] *adv*. 预先，事先

37. stowage ['stəʊɪdʒ] *n*. 贮藏

38. pilferage ['pɪlfəˌrɪdʒ] *n*. 偷盗

39. susceptible [sə'septəbl] *a*. 易受影响的

• •

1. be designed for   为……而设计

2. inner packing   内包装

3. outer packing   外包装

4. sales confirmation   成交确认书，销货确认，销售证明

5. international standard   国际标准

6. packing clause   包装条款

7. craft paper bag   牛皮纸袋

8. in addition   另外

9. seaworthy wooden case   适于航海的木箱

10. in transit   在路上，在途中

11. packing material   包装材料

12. forwarding agent   货运代理

13. in perfect condition   状况良好

14. be kept in mind   牢记在心

15. be divided into ...   被分为……

16. as small and light as possible   尽可能又小又轻

17. vary with ...   随着……的变化而变化

Unit 10

1. insurance [ɪn'ʃʊərəns] *n*. 保险

2. bother ['bɒðə] *v*. 麻烦，打扰

3. consideration [kənˌsɪdə'reɪʃən] *n*. 考虑

4. avoid [ə'vɔɪd] *v*. 避免

5. valid ['vælɪd] *a*. 有效的

6. compensation [ˌkɒmpən'seɪʃən] *n*. 赔偿

7. indemnity [ɪn'demnɪtɪ] *n*. 赔偿

8. average ['ævərɪdʒ] *n.* 平均

9. investigate [ɪn'vestɪgeɪt] *v.* 调查

10. principal ['prɪnsəpəl] *a.* 首要的,主要的

11. consignment [kən'saɪnmənt] *n.* 发货,委托

12. procedure [prə'siːdʒə] *n.* 程序,手续

13. seek [siːk] *v.* 寻找,探求

14. assess [ə'ses] *v.* 评估

15. premium ['priːmɪəm] *n.* 保险费

16. proof [pruːf] *n.* 证据

17. cover ['kʌvə] *v.* 投保各种保险

18. attach [ə'tætʃ] *v.* 附上,贴上

19. declaration [ˌdeklə'reɪʃən] *n.* 申报

• •

1. reach the destination   到达目的地

2. rough weather   恶劣的天气

3. suffer from   忍受,遭受

4. contract of indemnity   赔偿契约,赔偿合同

5. insurance policy   保险单

6. trade terms   贸易条款

7. mode of transport   运输模式

8. marine cargo insurance   海运货物保险

9. as far as   远到,直到,至于

10. basic type of risk   基本险

11. additional risk   附加险

12. proposal form   投保单

13. insurance certificate   保险凭证

14. floating policy   总保险单

15. open cover   预约保险单

16. cover note   暂保单

17. the insurer   保险者,保险公司

18. the insured   被保险者,保户

19. a sum of money   一笔款项

20. value policy   定值保险单

Unit 11

1. shipment ['ʃɪpmənt] *n.* 装船,运货

2. stage [steɪdʒ] *n.* 阶段,进程

3. consignor [kən'saɪnə] *n.* 委托人,发货人

国际商务英语函电

4. involve [ɪn'vɒlv] v. 牵涉，涉及
5. consignee [ˌkɒnsaɪ'ni:] n. 收货人，收件人
6. carrier ['kærɪə] n. 承运人
7. participate [pɑ:'tɪsɪpeɪt] v. 参与，参加
8. receipt [rɪ'si:t] n. 收据，收条
9. designate ['dezɪgneɪt] v. 指定
10. constitute ['kɒnstɪtju:t] v. 组成
11. convenience [kən'vi:njəns] n. 便利，方便
12. mode [məud] n. 模式，方式
13. combine [kəm'baɪn] v. 使联合
14. charter ['tʃɑ:tə] v. 租，包
15. procedure [prə'si:dʒə] n. 程序，手续
16. complex ['kɒmpleks] a. 复杂的
17. freight [freɪt] n. 运费，船
18. select [sɪ'lekt] v. 选择，挑选
19. vessel ['vesl] n. 船，舰
20. register ['redʒɪstə] v. 登记，记录
21. customs ['kʌstəmz] n. 海关
22. adequate ['ædɪkwɪt] n. 适当的，足够的
23. obtain [əb'teɪn] v. 获得，得到
24. intermediary [ˌɪntə'mi:dɪərɪ] n. 调解者，中间物
25. incline [ɪn'klaɪn] v. 使倾向于，使倾斜

• •

1. cover a wide range of work 包括大范围的工作
2. in some cases 在某些情况下
3. in case of 假设，万一
4. a large amount of goods 大批量货物
5. in several lots 分几批
6. sailing on different dates 于不同日期起航
7. call at 停靠
8. be allowed by 被……允许
9. in advance 提前，预先
10. be loaded on board a ship 被装在船上
11. in other words 换句话说
12. commercial invoice 商业发票
13. port of loading 装货港
14. port of destination 目的港
15. combined transport 联合运输
16. book shipping space 订舱位

17. take the form of either a Charter Party or a bill of lading　采用租船契约或提单的形式
18. find out freight rates　查明运费
19. shipping note　装运通知单
20. fill in the customs forms　填写海关单据
21. arrange adequate packing　安排合适的包装
22. advice note　通知单,通知书
23. consignment note　托运通知
24. forwarding agent　货代公司,运输行
25. the bank acting as intermediary　作为中间人的银行
26. be inclined to ...　倾向于……
27. (the goods) be cleared through the Customs　(货物)得以清关

Unit 12

1. complaint [kəmˈpleɪnt] n . 抱怨,投诉
2. inevitable [ɪnˈevɪtəbl] a . 不可避免的
3. ideal [aɪˈdɪəl] a . 理想的
4. supervise [ˈsjuːpəvaɪz] v . 监督
5. unfortunately [ʌnˈfɔːtʃənɪtlɪ] adv . 不幸地,遗憾地
6. error [ˈerə] n . 出错
7. occur [əˈkɜː] v . 发生,出现
8. mishandle [mɪsˈhændl] v . 错误地处理,胡乱操作
9. haste [heɪst] n . 匆忙,急忙
10. sufficiently [səˈfɪʃəntlɪ] adv . 充分地
11. unsatisfactory [ˌʌnsætɪsˈfæktərɪ] a . 令人不满意的
12. second-rate [ˈsekəndˈreɪt] a . 二流的
13. execution [ˌeksɪˈkjuːʃən] n . 执行
14. specify [ˈspesɪfaɪ] v . 指定,详细说明
15. face [feɪs] v . 面对
16. courteous [ˈkɜːtɪəs] a . 有礼貌的
17. unfounded [ʌnˈfaʊndɪd] a . 没有理由的
18. repudiate [rɪˈpjuːdɪeɪt] v . 批判,驳倒
19. reliable [rɪˈlaɪəbl] a . 可靠的
20. thoroughly [ˈθʌrəlɪ] adv . 彻底地
21. investigate [ɪnˈvestɪɡeɪt] v . 调查
22. solution [səˈluːʃən] n . 解决办法
23. reduction [rɪˈdʌkʃən] n . 减少,降低
24. determine [dɪˈtɜːmɪn] v . 决定
25. substantial [səbˈstænʃəl] a . 实质的
26. consequent [ˈkɒnsɪˌkwent] a . 随之发生的

国际商务英语函电

27. advantage [əd'vɑːntɪdʒ] *n*. 优势
28. advisable [əd'vaɪzəbl] *a*. 明智的
29. incur [ɪn'kɜː] *v*. 招致
30. compensation [ˌkɒmpən'seɪʃən] *n*. 补偿,赔偿
31. stoppage ['stɒpɪdʒ] *n*. 停止,填塞
32. concession [kən'seʃən] *n*. 让步

••••••••••••••••••••••••••••••••••••

1. complaining letter　投诉信
2. quality control　质量控制,质量管理
3. carry out　完成,实现,贯彻,执行
4. walk of life　行业,职业
5. work out　解决,算出
6. be mishandled　胡乱操作
7. as well as　也,又
8. lack of supervision　缺乏监督
9. a shortage of staff　缺乏员工
10. trained staff　训练有素的员工
11. arise from　起于
12. in right quantity　数量正确
13. second-rate product　二等产品
14. be dissatisfied with ...　对……不满
15. refer clearly to ...　清楚地指明……
16. the articles in question　上述产品
17. take action　采取行动
18. reply to complaint　回复投诉信
19. thoroughly investigate　彻底调查
20. suggest a solution　提出解决方案
21. agree to a price reduction　同意降价
22. the amount of the reduction　降价额
23. consequent loss　随之造成的损失
24. have the goods returned to ...　把货物返还给……
25. the added risk　增加风险
26. there is no need for *sb*. to do ...　对某人来说没必要做……
27. go into a long story　长篇大论
28. generally speaking　一般而言
29. have the matter put right　把事情做对

Appendix II   Phrases Commonly Used in Foreign Trade

1. Trade and Business
贸易与商务

world trade   世界贸易
barter trade   易货贸易
visible trade   有形贸易
invisible trade   无形贸易
trade fair / commodities trade   商品交易会
trade volume   贸易额
trade mark   商标
trade practice   贸易惯例
transit trade   过境贸易
trade representative   贸易代表
bilateral trade   双边贸易
compensation trade   补偿贸易
consignment transaction   寄售交易
counter trade   对销贸易
futures exchanges   期货交易所
futures trading / futures transaction   期货交易
general agent   总代理
import trade   进口贸易
multilateral trade   多边贸易
opening bidding   公开招标
processing trade   加工贸易
sale by sample   凭样销售
business discussion   贸易磋商
business hour   营业时间
business crisis   经营危机
banking business   银行业
business news   商业新闻
business service   商务服务

2. Business Negotiation
商务磋商

buying offer   买方发盘

国际商务英语函电

conditional acceptance　有条件接受
export contract　出口合同
import contract　进口合同
firm offer　实盘
enquiry sheet　询价单
invitation to make an offer　邀请发盘
late acceptance　逾期接受
non-firm offer　虚盘
order sheet　订单
sample order　看样订货
price sheet　价格表
purchase confirmation　购买确认书
purchase contract　购买合同
quotation sheet　报价单
reasonable time　合理时间
sales confirmation　销售确认书
sales contract　销售合同
sales note　售货单
purchase note　购货单
selling offer　卖方发盘
sign a contract　签订合同
trade agreement　贸易协定
voluntary offer　主动发盘
sufficiently definite　十分确定
with engagement　受约束
without engagement　不受约束

3. Price
价格

actual price　实际价格
agreement price　协议价
base price　基价
contracted price　合同价格
cost price　成本价
net price　净价
normal price　标准价格
reference price　参考价
retail price　零售价
spot price　现货价
total price　总价

unit price　单价
resale price　转售价
bottom price　底价
half price　半价
average price　平均价
price control　价格控制
reduce the price　减价
price war　价格战
raise the price　提价
favorable price　优惠价
workable price　可行的价格
current price　现价
moderate price　适中的价格
reasonable price　合理的价格
wholesale price　批发价

4. Quality，Weight and Measurement
货物质量、重量和尺码

description of goods　品名
detailed specification　详细的规格
specification of goods　商品规格
article number / item number　货号
grade of goods　商品等级
gross weight　毛重
gross for net　以毛作净
legal weight　法定重量
measurement ton　尺码吨
long ton　长吨
short ton　短吨
metric ton　公吨
net weight　净重
pattern sample　款式样
sale by grade　凭等级买卖
the metric system　公制
F. A. Q.（Fair Average Quality）　良好平均品质
sale by specification　凭规格买卖
sale by standard　凭标准买卖
quality as per buyer's sample　质量以买方样品为准
quality as per seller's sample　质量以卖方样品为准
sale by descriptions and illustrations　凭说明书和图样买卖

国际商务英语函电

5. Packing
包装

in bulk　散货

official marks　官方规定标志

customary packing／usual packing　习惯包装

export packing　出口包装

export standard packing　出口标准包装

improper packing　不良包装

designated packing　指定包装

marketing packing　销售包装

inner packing　内包装

neutral packing　中性包装

nude packed　裸装

outer packing　外包装

packing charges　包装费用

packing cost　包装成本

packing marks　包装标志

packing service　包装服务

packing specification　包装规格

particular packing　特定包装

seaworthy packing　适合海运的包装

airworthy packing　适合空运的包装

stencil shipping mark　唛唛头

usual packing　惯常包装

warning mark　警告性标志

waterproof packing　防水包装

6. Transportation
运输

air transport　航空运输

container transport　集装箱运输

freight prepaid／freight paid　运费已付

freight to be paid／freight to collect　运费到付

ocean transport／marine transport　海洋运输

optional port　选择港

partial shipment　分批装运

port of destination　目的港

port of shipment　起运港

port surcharge　港口附加费

rail transport　铁路运输

road transport　公路运输

running day　连续日

shipping advice　装运通知

shipping marks　唛头，装运标志

shipping documents　装运单据

shipping position　运输状况

shipping space　舱位

shipping instruction　装运指示

S/O（shipping order）　装货单

weight ton 重量吨

7. Documents
单据

air waybill　航空运单

bearer B/L　不记名提单

bill of lading　提单

clean B/L　清洁提单

combined transport B/L　多式联运提单

commercial invoice　商业发票

container B/L　集装箱提单

copy B/L　副本提单

C.T.D.（Combined Transport Documents）　多式联运单据

customs invoice　海关发票

direct shipped B/L　直达提单

on board B/L/shipped B/L　已装船提单

order B/L　指示提单

original B/L　正本提单

packing list　装箱单

received for shipped B/L　备运提单

straight B/L　记名提单

transhipment B/L　转船提单

unclean B/L/foul B/L　不清洁提单

weight memo　重量单

8. Insurance
保险

actual total loss　实际全损

All Risks　一切险

C.I.C.（China Insurance Clause）　保险条例

combined certificate　联合凭证

F. P. A.（Free from Particular Average）　平安险

F. W. R. D.（Fresh Water Rain Damage）　淡水雨淋险

G/A（General Average）　共同海损

G/A contribution　共同海损分摊

additional risks　附加险

general additional risks　一般附加险

Hook Damage　钩损险

I. C. C.（Institute Cargo Clause）　协会货物条款

insurance agent　保险代理

insurance certificate　保险凭证

insurance policy　保险单

insurance broker　保险经纪人

insurance claim　保险索赔

maritime charges　海上费用

natural calamities　自然灾害

open policy　预约保险单

P/A（Particular Average）　单独海损

PICC（the People's Insurance Company of China）　中国人民保险公司

Ocean Maritime Cargo Clause　海运货物保险条款

Risk of Leakage　渗漏险

Risk of Odor　串味险

Risk of Rust　锈损险

Risk of Shortage　短量险

salvage charges　救助费用

Strikes Risk　罢工险

sue and labor charges　施救费用

War Risk　战争险

W. P. A.（With Particular Average）　水渍险

W/W（Warehouse to Warehouse）　仓至仓条款

9. Payment
付款

bill of exchange　汇票

bona fide holder　持票人

clear bill　光票

clean credit　光票信用证

collecting bank　代收银行

commercial acceptance bill　商业承兑汇票

commercial draft　商业汇票

confirmed letter of credit 保兑信用证

confirming bank 保兑行

D/A（Documents Against Acceptance） 承兑交单

documentary bill 跟单汇票

documentary credit 跟单信用证

D/P（Documents Against Payment） 付款交单

D/P after sight 远期付款交单

D/P at sight 即期付款交单

L/C（Letter of Credit） 信用证

irrevocable letter of credit 不可撤销信用证

M/T（Mail Transfer） 信汇

money order 汇款单

negotiating bank 议付行

negotiation credit 议付信用证

non-transferable L/C 不可转让信用证

opening bank/issuing bank 开证行

paying bank/drawee bank 付款行

payment by installments 分期付款

payment credit 付款信用证

payment in advance 预付货款

performance guarantee 履约保证函

presenting bank 提示行

promissory note 本票

remitting bank 托收行

revocable letter of credit 可撤销信用证

sight credit 即期信用证

sight draft 即期汇票

time draft（usance bill） 远期汇票

draw a draft 开立汇票

T/T（Telegraphic Transfer） 电汇

transferable credit 可转让信用证

T/R（Trust Receipt） 信托收据

UCP500 跟单信用证统一惯例

URC522 国际商会第 522 号出版物

unconfirmed letter of credit 不可保兑信用证

usance letter of credit 远期信用证

10. Inspection
检验

Inspection Certificate of Health 卫生检验证书

国际商务英语函电

Inspection Certificate of Origin　产地检验证书
Inspection Certificate of Quality　品质检验证书
Inspection Certificate of Quantity　数量检验证书
Inspection Certificate of Weight　重量检验证书
Inspection Certificate of Value　价值检验证书
Inspection Certificate of Damaged Cargo　验残证书
Veterinary Inspection Certificate　兽医检验证书
Inspection Certificate of Tank/Hold　验舱证书
Commodity Inspection Bureau　商品检验局

Appendix III   Incoterms 2010 & 2000

《2010 年国际贸易术语解释通则》（International Rules for the Interpretation of Trade Terms 2010，缩写 Incoterms® 2010，以下称 2010 通则）是国际商会根据国际货物贸易的发展，对《2000 年国际贸易术语解释通则》（以下简称 2000 通则）的修订，于 2010 年 9 月 27 日公布，2011 年 1 月 1 日实施，它与《2000 年国际贸易术语解释通则》的主要区别是删去了 4 个术语，添加了 2 个术语，并进行了一些改动，具体内容如下。

一、删除 4 个术语，新增 2 个术语

2010 通则删去了 2000 通则中的 4 个术语：DAF（Delivered at Frontier）边境交货、DES（Delivered Ex Ship）目的港船上交货、DEQ（Delivered Ex Quay）目的港码头交货、DDU（Delivered Duty Unpaid）未完税交货；新增了 2 个术语：DAT（Delivered at Terminal）在指定目的地或目的港的集散站交货、DAP（Delivered at Place）在指定目的地交货。即用 DAP 取代了 DAF、DES 和 DDU 三个术语，用 DAT 取代了 DEQ，且扩展至适用于一切运输方式。2010 通则有 11 个术语，而 2000 通则有 13 个术语。

DAT（Delivered at Terminal）在指定目的地或目的港的集散站交货，指卖方在指定目的地或目的港的集散站卸货后将货物交给买方处置即完成交货，术语所指目的地包括港口。卖方应承担货物运至指定的目的地或目的港的集散站的一切风险和费用（除进口费用外）。本术语适用于任何运输方式或多式联运。

DAP（Delivered at Place）在指定目的地交货，指卖方在指定目的地交货，只需做好卸货准备而无需卸货即完成交货。术语所指的到达车辆包括船舶，目的地包括港口。卖方应承担将货物运至指定目的地的一切风险和费用（除进口费用外）。本术语适用于任何运输方式或多式联运及海运。

二、采用"两类分类法"取代"EFCD"

2010 通则共有 11 个贸易术语，按照所适用的运输方式划分为两大类（而之前的版本分为 E、F、C、D 四组）。

第一组：适用于任何运输方式的术语七种：**EXW、FCA、CPT、CIP、DAT、DAP、DDP**。

EXW（Ex Works） 工厂交货；

FCA（Free Carrier） 货交承运人；

CPT（Carriage Paid to） 运费付至目的地；

CIP（Carriage and Insurance Paid to） 运费保险费付至目的地；

DAT（Delivered at Terminal） 目的地或目的港的集散站交货；

DAP（Delivered at Place） 目的地交货；

DDP（Delivered Duty Paid） 完税后交货。

第二组：适用于水上运输方式的术语四种：**FAS、FOB、CFR、CIF**。

FAS（Free Alongside） 装运港船边交货；

FOB（Free on Board） 装运港船上交货；

CFR（Cost and Freight） 成本加运费；

CIF（Cost Insurance and Freight ） 成本、保险费加运费。

国际商务英语函电

References

1. 全国外贸中等专业学校教材编写组（1993），对外经贸英语函电，对外经济贸易大学出版社
2. Franz Sester Elfriede Seter（1999），商界英语，外语教学与研究出版社
3. Lan W，Catrin L－J，Anne W（2002），新编剑桥商务英语（第二版），经济科学出版社
4. Sue R（2003），新视野商务英语（上），外语教学与研究出版社
5. Graham T，Tonya T（2004），新视野商务英语（下），外语教学与研究出版社
6. Leo J，Richard A（2003），剑桥国际商务英语，华夏出版社
7. 程同春（2005），新编国际商务英语函电，东南大学出版社
8. 李倩春（2005），商务英语函电实训，对外经济贸易大学出版社
9. 胡鉴明（2004），商务英语函电，中国商务出版社
10. 滕美荣　许楠（2005），外贸英语函电，首都经济贸易大学出版社
11. 杨国俊　邱革加（2003），商务英语读写教程，北京航空航天大学出版社
12. 仲鑫（2006），外贸函电，机械工业出版社
13. 王兴孙（2007），新编进出口英语函电，上海交通大学出版社
14. 冯祥春（2008），新编大学国际商务英语函电教程，中国商务出版社
15. 冯祥春（2007），外经贸英语函电，对外经济贸易大学出版社
16. 房玉靖（2009），商务英语函电，清华大学出版社
17. 冼燕华（2006），国际商务英语函电，暨南大学出版社
18. 郝美彦（2010），外贸英文函电，东北财经大学出版社
19. 周琳（2010），外贸英语函电，上海财经大学出版社
20. 贾和平　黄梨　赵曙亚（2010），外贸英语函电，经济科学出版社
21. Michelle Witte　罗慕谦（2011），英文商务书信，华东理工大学出版社
22. 兰天　时敏　叶富国（2010），外贸英语函电，科学出版社
23. 曲继武　赵树　程有义（2010），外贸函电实战技巧，广东经济出版社
24. 赵银德（2010），外贸函电，机械工业出版社
25. David Clarke（2011），高级商务信函，北京大学出版社
26. 郭琛（2010），外贸英语函电，哈尔滨工程大学出版社
27. 侯方淼（2010），外贸英语函电，电子工业出版社
28. 赵春漫（2011），外贸英语函电，北京大学出版社
29. 喆儒（2011），现代国际商务函电，人民邮电出版社
30. 殷秀玲（2011），外贸函电，立信会计出版社
31. 林涛　姜丽（2011），国际商务英文与函电，清华大学出版社
32. 郑敏（2005），商务英语函电与合同，清华大学出版社，北京交通大学出版社
33. 金双玉　钦寅（2006），外贸英语——函电与单证，同济大学出版社
34. 黄振华（2010），商务英语函电，中国财政经济出版社

国际商务英语函电

35. 刘志伟(2011),国际商务函电,对外贸易大学出版社
36. 郑黎明(2011),外贸函电,西安交通大学出版社
37. 郑书燕(2010),新编商务英语函电,对外经济贸易大学出版社
38. 程同春　程欣(2012),新编商务英语函电,东南大学出版社

图书在版编目(CIP)数据

国际商务英语函电/沙佩主编. —上海:华东师范大学
出版社,2012.11
ISBN 978 - 7 - 5675 - 0049 - 5

Ⅰ.①国… Ⅱ.①沙… Ⅲ.①国际贸易-英语-电报
信函-写作-中等专业学校-教材 Ⅳ.①H315

中国版本图书馆 CIP 数据核字(2012)第 262000 号

国际商务英语函电

职业学校商贸、财经专业教学用书

主　编　沙　佩
责任编辑　李　琴
审读编辑　蒋　雯
装帧设计　徐颖超

出　　版　华东师范大学出版社
社　　址　上海市中山北路 3663 号
　　　　　邮编 200062

营销策划　上海龙智文化咨询有限公司
电　　话　021 - 51698271　51698272
传　　真　021 - 51698271

印 刷 者　常熟市文化印刷有限公司
开　　本　787×1092　16 开
印　　张　10.25
字　　数　220 千字
版　　次　2012 年 12 月第 1 版
印　　次　2015 年 10 月第 2 次
书　　号　ISBN 978-7-5675-0049-5/G·5991
定　　价　20.00 元

出版人　王　焰

(如发现本版图书有印订质量问题,请与华东师范大学出版社联系
电话:021-51698271　51698272)